BE

RICH

GAINING THE THINGS THAT MONEY CAN'T BUY

NT COMMENTARY

EPHESIANS

Warren W. Wiersbe

David C Cook

transforming lives together

BE RICH
Published by David C Cook
4050 Lee Vance Drive
Colorado Springs, CO 80918 U.S.A.

David C Cook U.K., Kingsway Communications
Eastbourne, East Sussex BN23 6NT, England

The graphic circle C logo is a registered trademark of David C Cook.

Unless otherwise noted, all Scripture quotations are taken from the King James Version of the Bible. (Public Domain.) Scripture quotations marked NASB are taken from the *New American Standard Bible*, © Copyright 1960, 1995 by The Lockman Foundation. Used by permission; NIV are taken from the *Holy Bible, New International Version*®. NIV®. Copyright © 1973, 1978, 1984 International Bible Society. Used by permission of Zondervan. All rights reserved; WMS are taken from The New Testament in the Language of the People by Charles B. Williams, © 1966 by Edith S. Williams. Used by permission of Moody Press, Moody Bible Institute of Chicago; and TLB are taken from *The Living Bible*, © 1971, Tyndale House Publishers, Wheaton, IL 60189. Used by permission.

LCCN 2008937432
ISBN 978-1-4347-6732-5
eISBN 978-1-4347-6450-8

First edition of *Be Rich* by Warren W. Wiersbe published by Victor Books®
in 1979 © Warren W. Wiersbe, ISBN 978-0-89693-775-8

The Team: Karen Lee-Thorp, Amy Kiechlin, Jack Campbell, and Susan Vannaman
Series Cover Design: John Hamilton Design
Cover Photo: iStockphoto

Printed in the United States of America
Second Edition 2009

13 14 15 16 17 18 19 20 21 22

102317

BE

RICH

Dedicated with appreciation
to my predecessors at
The Moody Church, Chicago
Dr. S. Franklin Logsdon
Dr. Alan Redpath
Dr. H. A. Hermansen
Dr. George Sweeting

Other men laboured, and ye are entered into their labours.
—John 4:38

CONTENTS

The Big Idea

An Introduction to *Be Rich*
by Ken Baugh

Before my wife Susan met me, she was dating a billionaire's son. Yes, you read that right: *billionaire*. So as you can imagine, money was never an issue. In fact, if she had married this guy, she would have been set for life, at least financially. Can you imagine never having to worry about money? Never having to say no to anything, never having to be on a budget? You could buy whatever you wanted—sports cars, boats, planes, you name it. If you married into a billionaire family, you would be on the invite list to all the exclusive parties, you would be able to take exotic vacations and travel the world in Learjets and aboard private yachts. It sounds pretty nice, especially if things are tough for you financially.

Thankfully—for me at least—instead of marrying a billionaire she married a guy who was at that time a wannabe pastor. When I met her, twenty-three years ago, I had maybe $150 to my name, and I was driving a 1979 Datsun B-210 hatchback with chrome-spoked rims and sheepskin seat covers. I didn't have much. It's true that Susan and I have never had a lot of money, but it's also true that we have never been in need of much either. God has *always* been faithful to provide for our needs above and beyond what we ever imagined.

Over the last twenty years as a pastor I have met a lot of very wealthy people, and if there is one thing I have learned as I have watched the rich and famous from the sidelines, it is that money doesn't buy happiness. Money doesn't bring peace or security. Money is here today and lost in the stock market tomorrow. There is only one source of true wealth, only one means of lasting peace and security, and that is being in Christ. In fact, the Big Idea in Paul's letter to the church in Ephesus is that every Christian is rich in Christ.

"In Christ" is the most frequently used phrase in the book of Ephesians, and the point is clear: If you're in Christ, you have everything. For example, Christians are saints in Christ (1:1); blessed in Christ (1:3); chosen in Christ (1:4); adopted by Christ (1:5); lavished with love in Christ (1:6); redeemed and forgiven in Christ (1:7); participants in God's good plan in Christ (1:11); glorified in Christ, sealed with the Holy Spirit (1:12–13); made alive in Christ (2:5–6); created in Christ (2:10); brought near to God in Christ (2:13); growing in Christ (2:21); built in Christ (2:22); and sharers in God's promise in Christ (3:6). Get the picture? Everything in the universe is centered in Christ (1:10).

As a Christian you are in Christ, and being in Christ simply means that you are part of the family of God. You're so wealthy, it makes a billionaire family seem like paupers.

How this can be true? How is it possible to be in the family of the King of the Universe? That is a great question, and the answer will change how you look at your life forever. Paul tells us in Ephesians 1:4–5 that every Christian is adopted into God's family. "In love he predestined us to be adopted as his sons through Jesus Christ" (NIV). Don't miss this great truth: As a Christian you are an adopted son or daughter of God. That makes you royalty, a prince or princess of the King of the Universe.

In my opinion this is one of the most life-changing truths found in

Scripture. In Paul's day an adopted child had all the rights and privileges of a natural born son or daughter. The Roman judicial system recognized an adopted child as a new person. All your debts and obligations from your former life were wiped out. As an adopted child of God, you have a fresh start, a new beginning, a totally new life. Look at what the Bible says about this:

> Now we are no longer slaves but God's own sons. And since we are his sons, everything he has belongs to us. (Gal. 4:7 TLB)

> And since we are his children, we will share his treasures—for all God gives to his Son Jesus is now ours too. (Rom. 8:17 TLB)

> You will live, because those who are led by the Spirit of God are sons of God. For you did not receive a spirit that makes you a slave again to fear, but you received the Spirit of sonship. And by him we cry, "Abba, Father." The Spirit himself testifies with our spirit that we are God's children. Now if we are children, then we are heirs—heirs of God and co-heirs with Christ. (Rom. 8:14–17)

Let me list for you some of the benefits of our inheritance in Jesus Christ as adopted children of God.

The first benefit is that we become part of God's family, and every other believer becomes our brother and sister. If you're an only child, now you have a ton of siblings and you're not alone any longer. So be nice to those people you go to church with; you are going to be with them for eternity!

The second benefit is that each of us has a unique and intimate relationship with God. You can actually call Him "Daddy." That's what *Abba* means. God loves you as a "daddy." He loves His children, and He wants to provide for you, and comfort and encourage you as your daddy. Dr. Wayne Grudem reminds us that "the role that is most intimate, and the role that conveys the highest privileges of fellowship with God for eternity, is his role as our heavenly Father" (*Systematic Theology*, 739).

The third benefit is that every believer is an heir with Jesus to everything that God owns. During the first century, an adopted son of a wealthy man would be given his signet ring, which in essence was a black American Express card that he could use to purchase anything. (It's actually called the Centurion Card and arrives at your house carried by a security guard and contained in a velvet-lined box. It includes a special mini-computer and two black cards, one for pleasure and one for business.) If you sealed a deed with your adopted father's signet ring, the deal was binding. The ring also served as a visible sign to all who would see it on your finger that you were your father's child.

The fourth benefit is that every believer has a privileged position that will continue into eternity. No angel or any other created being will share your status as one of God's children. Jesus said, "To him who overcomes, I will give the right to sit with me on my throne, just as I overcame and sat down with my Father on his throne" (Rev. 3:21).

The fifth benefit is that every believer will rule the nations with Christ during the millennial kingdom. And I could go on and on and tell you about how as an adopted child of God you will receive a new heavenly body, that you are no longer under the wrath of God, that you have an eternal home in heaven. Perhaps the greatest truth is that you cannot loose this status. Once you trust Jesus Christ as your Savior, you are "marked in him with a seal, the promised Holy Spirit, who is a deposit guaranteeing our inheritance" (Eph. 1:13–14).

Do you get it yet? In Christ you are rich! What a glorious, life-changing, behavior-altering, thought-provoking truth.

I hope that as you read Dr. Wiersbe's commentary, you will be renewed in your thinking and refreshed in your spirit because of your privileged status as an adopted child of God. My prayer for you is the same as Paul's: "I pray also that the eyes of your heart may be enlightened in order that you may know the hope to which he has called you, the riches of his glorious inheritance in the saints, and his incomparably great power for us who believe" (Eph. 1:18–19).

***

Dr. Wiersbe's commentaries have been a source of guidance and strength to me over the many years that I have been a pastor. His unique style is not overly academic, but theologically sound. He unpacks the deep truths of Scripture in a way that everyone can understand and apply. Whether you're a Bible scholar or a brand-new believer in Christ, you will benefit, as I have, from Warren's insights. With your Bible in one hand and Dr. Wiersbe's commentary in the other, you will be able to accurately unpack the deep truths of God's Word and learn how to apply them to your life.

Drink deeply, my friend, of the truths of God's Word, for in them you will find Jesus Christ, and there is freedom, peace, assurance, and joy.

—Ken Baugh
Pastor of Coast Hills Community Church
Aliso Viejo, California

A WORD FROM THE AUTHOR

A story I heard years ago pretty well sums up what I say in this book.

An undernourished boy was found on the city street and taken to a hospital. After the nurses had bathed him and dressed him, they put him to bed and brought him his dinner tray. Conspicuous on that tray was a large glass of milk. The boy's eyes lit up as he reached for the glass, but then he paused and, looking at the nurses, asked a question that broke their hearts:

"Can I drink *all* of it?"

It was obvious that back home there was never enough of anything. It makes me think of the woman who stood watching the Atlantic Ocean and said, "It sure is good to see something that there's plenty of!"

Too many Christians are living like paupers when Christ has made us rich! Isn't it time we stopped living on substitutes (even *religious* substitutes) and started drawing on the riches we have in Christ?

My friend—*Be Rich*!

—Warren W. Wiersbe

A Suggested Outline of the Book of Ephesians

Theme: The believer's riches in Christ
Key verse: Ephesians 1:3

I. Doctrine: Our Riches in Christ (Ephesians 1—3)
    A. Our spiritual possessions in Christ (Ephesians 1:4–14)
        1. From the Father (Ephesians 1:4–6)
        2. From the Son (Ephesians 1:7–12)
        3. From the Spirit (Ephesians 1:13–14)
    First Prayer—for enlightenment (Ephesians 1:15–23)
    B. Our spiritual position in Christ (Ephesians 2:1–22)
        1. Raised and seated on the throne (Ephesians 2:1–10)
        2. Reconciled and set into the temple (Ephesians 2:11–22)
    Second Prayer—for enablement (Ephesians 3:1–21) (vv. 2–13 are
    a parenthesis)
II. Duty: Our Responsibilities in Christ (Ephesians 4—6)
    A. Walk in unity (Ephesians 4:1–16)
    B. Walk in purity (Ephesians 4:17—5:17)
        1. Walk not as other Gentiles (Ephesians 4:17–32)
        2. Walk in love (Ephesians 5:1–6)
        3. Walk as children of light (Ephesians 5:7–14)
        4. Walk carefully (Ephesians 5:15–17)
    C. Walk in harmony (Ephesians 5:18—6:9)
        1. Husbands and wives (Ephesians 5:18–33)
        2. Parents and children (Ephesians 6:1–4)
        3. Masters and servants (Ephesians 6:5–9)
    D. Walk in victory (Ephesians 6:10–24)

Chapter One

SAINTS ALIVE!

(Ephesians 1:1–3)

S he had gone down in history as "America's Greatest Miser," yet when she died in 1916, "Hetty" Green left an estate valued at over $100 million. She ate cold oatmeal because it cost to heat it. Her son had to suffer a leg amputation, because she delayed so long in looking for a free clinic that his case became incurable. She was wealthy, yet she chose to live like a pauper.

Eccentric? Certainly! Crazy? Perhaps—but nobody could prove it. She was so foolish that she hastened her own death by bringing on an attack of apoplexy while arguing about the value of drinking skimmed milk! But Hetty Green is an illustration of too many Christian believers today. They have limitless wealth at their disposal, and yet they live like paupers. It was to this kind of Christian that Paul wrote the epistle to the Ephesians.

THE AUTHOR (1:1A)

Some names in history we identify immediately, and "Paul" is one of them. His name was originally "Saul" (Acts 7:58), and, since he was from the tribe of Benjamin (Phil. 3:5), it is likely he was named after the first king of Israel (1 Sam. 9). Unlike his namesake, however, Saul of Tarsus was obedient, and faithfully served God. As a devoted rabbi, Saul became the leader of the anti-Christian movement in Jerusalem (Acts 9:1–2; Gal. 1:13–14). But in the midst of this activity, Saul was "arrested" by Jesus Christ and was converted (Acts 9:3ff.; 26).

Saul of Tarsus became Paul, the apostle to the Gentiles (Acts 9:15). While he was ministering in the church of Antioch, he was called by the Spirit to take the gospel to the Gentiles, and he obeyed (Acts 13:1–3). The book of Acts records three missionary journeys that took Paul throughout the Roman Empire in one of the greatest evangelistic endeavors in church history. About the year 53, Paul first ministered in Ephesus but did not remain there (Acts 18:19–21). Two years later, while on his third journey, Paul stayed in Ephesus for at least two years and saw that whole vast area evangelized (Acts 19:1–20). During these years, he founded a strong church in the city that was dedicated to the worship of the goddess Diana. For a description of Paul's ministry in Ephesus, read Acts 20, and for an explanation of the opposition to Paul's ministry there, read Acts 19:21–41.

It was nearly ten years later when Paul wrote to his beloved friends in Ephesus. Paul was a prisoner in Rome (Eph. 3:1; 4:1; 6:20), and he wanted to share with these believers the great truths the Lord had taught him about Christ and the church. Compare Ephesians 6:21–22 with Colossians 4:7–9 and Philemon to get a better understanding of the historical background. Onesimus, a slave, ran away from Philemon, his master, who lived at Colossae. While in Rome, Onesimus met Paul and was converted. Tychicus, one of the pastors of the church at Colossae, which may have met in Philemon's house, was also in Rome to discuss some problems with Paul. So Paul took advantage of the presence of these two men to send three letters to his friends: the epistle to the Ephesians, the epistle to the Colossians, and the epistle to Philemon. At the same time, he sent Onesimus back to his master.

So, the letter was written from Rome about the year AD 62. Though Paul was on trial for his life, he was concerned about the spiritual needs of the churches he had founded. As an *apostle,* "one sent with a commission," he had an obligation to teach them the Word of God and to seek to build them up in the faith (Eph. 4:11–12).

THE ASSEMBLY (1:1B–2)

Are you surprised to find Paul addressing his letter to *saints?* After all, saints are dead people who have achieved such spiritual eminence that they have been given that special title, *saints.* Or are they?

No word in the New Testament has suffered more than this word *saint.* Even the dictionary defines a *saint* as a "person officially recognized for holiness of life." Who makes this official recognition? Usually some religious body, and the process by which a person becomes a saint is technically known as *canonization.* The deceased person's life is examined carefully to see whether he qualifies for sainthood. If the candidate's character and conduct are found to be above reproach, if he has been responsible for working at least two miracles, then he is qualified to be made a saint.

As interesting as this procedure is, we do not find it authorized in the Bible. Nine times in this brief letter, Paul addressed his readers as saints (Eph. 1:1, 15, 18; 2:19; 3:8, 18; 4:12; 5:3; 6:18). These saints were alive, not dead, though once they had been "dead in trespasses and sins" (Eph. 2:1–3). And it is clear that they had never performed any miracles, though they had *experienced* a miracle by trusting Christ as Savior (Eph. 2:4–10). The word *saint* is simply one of the many terms used in the New Testament to describe "one who has trusted Jesus Christ as Savior." The person is "alive," not only physically, but also spiritually (Eph. 2:1). You will find Christians called *disciples* (Acts 9:1, 10, 19, 25–26, 36, 38), *people of the Way* (Acts 9:2), and *saints* (Acts 9:13, 32, 41).

The word *saint* means "one who has been set apart." It is related to the word *sanctified*, which means "set apart." When the sinner trusts Christ as his Savior, he is taken out of "the world" and placed "in Christ." The believer is *in* the world physically, but not of the world spiritually (John 17:14–16). Like a scuba diver, he exists in an alien environment because he possesses special equipment—in this case, the indwelling Holy Spirit of God. Every true believer possesses the Holy Spirit (Rom. 8:9; 1 Cor. 6:19–20), and it is through the Spirit's power that the Christian is able to function in the world.

Now for the important question: How did these people at Ephesus become saints? The answer is found in two words: "faithful" and "grace" (Eph. 1:1–2). When Paul addressed his letter to the "saints … and faithful in Christ Jesus" he was not addressing two different groups of people. The word *faithful* carries the meaning of "believers in Christ Jesus." These people were not saved by living faithful lives; rather they put their faith in Christ and were saved. This is clear from Ephesians 1:12–14, 19.

The word *grace* is used twelve times in Ephesians and refers to "the kindness of God toward undeserving people." Grace and mercy often are found together in the Bible, and they certainly belong together in the experience of salvation. *Grace* and *faith* go together, because the only way to experience grace and salvation is through faith (Eph. 2:8–9).

The phrase "in Christ Jesus" is used twenty-seven times in this letter! It describes the spiritual position of the believer: He is identified with Christ. He is in Christ, and therefore is able to draw on the wealth of Christ for his own daily living.

THE AIM (1:3)

Each book in the Bible has its own special theme and message, even though it may deal with many different topics. Genesis is the book of *beginnings;*

Matthew is the book of the *kingdom;* Galatians is the book of *liberty.* Ephesians 1:3 states its theme: *the Christian's riches in Christ.*

The source of our blessings. "Blessed be the God and Father of our Lord Jesus Christ." God the Father has made us rich in Jesus Christ! When you were born again into God's family, you were born rich. Through Christ you share in the riches of God's grace (Eph. 1:7; 2:7), God's glory (Eph. 1:18; 3:16), God's mercy (Eph. 2:4), and "the unsearchable riches of Christ" (Eph. 3:8). Our heavenly Father is not poor; He is rich—and He has made us rich in His Son.

J. Paul Getty, one of the richest men in the world, was worth an estimated $1.3 billion. The weekly income of some of the "oil sheiks" runs into the millions. Yet all of this wealth is but "pennies" when compared with the spiritual wealth we have in Christ. In this letter, Paul explained to us what these riches are and how we may draw on them for effective Christian living.

The scope of our blessings. We have "all spiritual blessings." This can be translated "all the blessings of the Spirit," referring to the Holy Spirit of God. In the Old Testament, God promised His earthly people, Israel, material blessings as a reward for their obedience (Deut. 28:1–13). Today, He promises to supply all our needs "according to his riches in glory by Christ Jesus" (Phil. 4:19), but He does not promise to shield us from either poverty or pain. The Father has given us every blessing of the Spirit, everything we need for a successful, satisfying Christian life. *The spiritual is far more important than the material.*

The Holy Spirit is mentioned many times in this letter, because He is the One who channels our riches to us from the Father, through the Son. Not to know and depend on the Holy Spirit's provision is to live a life of spiritual poverty. No wonder Paul began his Ephesian ministry asking some professed Christians if they really knew the Holy Spirit (Acts 19:1–7). We might ask professed Christians today, "Did you receive the Holy Spirit when you believed?" If the answer is no, then you are not saved. "Now if any man have not the Spirit of Christ, he is none of his" (Rom. 8:9). Unless you have the *witness* of the Spirit (Rom. 8:15–16), you cannot draw on the *wealth* of the Spirit.

The sphere of our blessings. Our blessings are "in heavenly places in Christ." Perhaps a clearer translation would be "in the heavenlies in Christ." The unsaved person is interested primarily in *earthlies,* because this is where he lives. Jesus called them "the children of this world" (Luke 16:8). The Christian's life is centered in *heaven.* His citizenship is in heaven (Phil. 3:20); his name is written in heaven (Luke 10:20); his Father is in heaven; and his attention and affection ought to be centered on the things of heaven (Col. 3:1ff.). Evangelist D. L. Moody used to warn about people who were so "heavenly minded they were no earthly good," but that is not what Paul was describing. "The heavenlies" (literal translation) describes that place where Jesus Christ is right now (Eph. 1:2) and where the believer is seated with Him (Eph. 2:6). The battles we fight are not with flesh and blood on earth, but with satanic powers "in the heavenlies" (Eph. 6:12).

The Christian really operates in two spheres: the human and the divine, the visible and the invisible. Physically, he is on the earth in a human body, but spiritually he is seated with Christ in the heavenly sphere—and it is this heavenly sphere that provides the power and direction for the earthly walk. The president of the United States is not always seated at his desk in the White House, but that executive chair represents the sphere of his life and power. No matter where he is, he is the president, because only he has the privilege of sitting at that desk. Likewise with the Christian: No matter where he may be on this earth, he is seated in the heavenlies with Jesus Christ, and this is the basis of his life and power.

When she was young, Victoria was shielded from the fact that she would be the next ruling monarch of England lest this knowledge spoil her. When her teacher finally did let her discover for herself that she would one day be Queen of England, Victoria's response was, "Then I will be good!" Her life would be controlled by her position. No matter where she was, Victoria was governed by the fact that she sat on the throne of England.

The fact that Paul is writing about wealth would be significant to his readers, because Ephesus was considered the bank of Asia. One of the seven wonders of the world—the great temple of Diana—was in Ephesus and was not only a center for idolatrous worship, but also a depository for wealth. Some of the greatest art treasures of the ancient world were housed in this magnificent building. In this letter, Paul will compare the church of Jesus Christ to a temple and will explain the great wealth that Christ has in His church. Paul has already used the word *riches*, but you may want to check other "financial" words such as *inheritance* (Eph. 1:11, 14, 18; 5:5) and *fullness*, or *filled* (Eph. 1:10, 23; 3:19; 4:10, 13; 5:18). Paul is saying to us, "*Be Rich!*"

The Analysis

Paul's letter to the Ephesians is as carefully structured as that great temple of Diana, and it contains greater beauty and wealth! We *inherit* the wealth by faith and *invest* the wealth by works. Without this balance, our spiritual riches do us no good.

QUESTIONS FOR PERSONAL REFLECTION
OR GROUP DISCUSSION

1. If you were rich, how would your life be different?

2. What do you think it means to be spiritually rich?

3. Read Ephesians 1:1–3. Why does Paul identify his readers as "saints"?

4. Is it helpful for you to think of yourself as a saint? Explain.

5. For Paul, living "in Christ" is a more significant aspect of your identity than living "in Ephesus" or "in America" or "in the South" or "in the suburbs." How is your life affected by where you live geographically?

6. How does living "in Christ" affect who you are and how you live?

7. What do you know about the heavenly sphere of reality?

8. How much do you think about the heavenly sphere of reality on a typical day? Why is that?

9. How do we get "all spiritual blessings"?

10. What can you do to gain all that Christ has for you as you study Ephesians?

Chapter Two

How Rich You Are!

(Ephesians 1:4–14)

One of the funniest cartoons I ever saw showed a pompous lawyer reading a client's last will and testament to a group of greedy relatives. The caption read, "I, John Jones, being of sound mind and body, *spent it all!*"

When Jesus Christ wrote His last will and testament for His church, He made it possible for us to share His spiritual riches. Instead of spending it all, Jesus Christ paid it all. His death on the cross and His resurrection make possible our salvation.

He wrote us into His will, then He died so the will would be in force. Then He arose again that He might become the heavenly Advocate (lawyer) to make sure the terms of the will were correctly followed!

In this long sentence, Paul named just a few of the blessings that make up our spiritual wealth.

Blessings from God the Father (1:4–6)

He has chosen us (v. 4). This is the marvelous doctrine of *election,* a doctrine that has confused some and confounded others. A seminary professor once said to me, "Try to explain election and you may lose your mind.

But try to explain it away and you may lose your soul!" That salvation begins with God, and not with man, all Christians will agree. "Ye have not chosen me, but I have chosen you" (John 15:16). The lost sinner, left to his own ways, does not seek God (Rom. 3:10–11); God in His love seeks the sinner (Luke 19:10).

Note that God chose us even before He created the universe, so that our salvation is wholly of His grace and not on the basis of anything we ourselves have done. He chose us *in Christ,* not in ourselves. And He chose us for a purpose: to be holy and without blame. In the Bible, election is always *unto* something. It is a privilege that carries a great responsibility.

Does the sinner respond to God's grace against his own will? No, he responds because God's grace makes him willing to respond. The mystery of divine sovereignty and human responsibility will never be solved in this life. Both are taught in the Bible (John 6:37). Both are true, and both are essential.

You will note that all three persons in the Godhead are involved in our salvation (see also 1 Peter 1:3). As far as God the Father is concerned, you were saved when He chose you in Christ in eternity past. But that alone did not save you. As far as God the Son is concerned, you were saved when He died for you on the cross. As far as God the Spirit is concerned, you were saved when you yielded to His conviction and received Christ as your Savior. What began in eternity past was fulfilled in time present, and will continue for all eternity!

He has adopted us (v. 5). Here we meet that misunderstood word *predestination.* This word, as it is used in the Bible, refers *primarily* to what God does for saved people. Nowhere in the Bible are we taught that people are predestined to hell, because this word refers only to God's people. The word simply means "to ordain beforehand, to predetermine." Election seems to refer to *people,* while predestination refers to *purposes.* The events connected with the crucifixion of Christ were predestined (Acts 4:25–28). God has predestined our adoption (Eph. 1:5) and our conformity to Christ (Rom. 8:29–30), as well as our future inheritance (Eph. 1:11).

Adoption has a dual meaning, both present and future. You do not get into God's family by adoption. You get into His family by regeneration, the new birth (John 3:1–18; 1 Peter 1:22–25). Adoption is the act of God by which He gives His "born ones" an adult standing in the family. Why does He do this? So that we might *immediately* begin to claim our inheritance and enjoy our spiritual wealth! A baby cannot legally use this inheritance (Gal. 4:1–7), but an adult son can—and should! This means that you do not have to wait until you are an old saint before you can claim your riches in Christ.

The *future* aspect of adoption is found in Romans 8:22–23, the glorified body we will have when Jesus returns. We already have our adult standing before God, but the world cannot see this. When Christ returns, this "private adoption" will be made public for everyone to see!

He has accepted us (v. 6). We cannot make ourselves acceptable to God, but He, by His grace, makes us accepted in Christ. This is our eternal position that will never change. Some translations read "which He freely bestowed on us in the Beloved" (NASB). Or, "He has *be-graced* [literal translation] us in the Beloved." The idea is the same. Because of God's grace in Christ, we are accepted before Him. Paul wrote Philemon to encourage him to accept his runaway slave, Onesimus, using the same argument. "If he owes you anything, I will pay it. Receive him as you would receive me" (Philem. 17–19, paraphrased). The parallel is easy to see.

BLESSINGS FROM GOD THE SON (1:7–12)

We should not think that each person of the Godhead works independently, because they all worked together to make possible our salvation. But each Person has a special ministry to perform, a special "spiritual deposit" to make in our lives.

He has redeemed us (v. 7a). To *redeem* means "to purchase and set free by paying a price." There were sixty million slaves in the Roman Empire, and often they were bought and sold like pieces of furniture. But a man could purchase a slave and set him free, and this is what Jesus did for us. The price was His own blood (1 Peter 1:18ff.). This means that we are free from the law (Gal. 5:1), free from slavery to sin (Rom. 6), as well as free from the power of Satan and the world (Gal. 1:4; Col. 1:13–14). If we were slaves, we would be poor, but because we are sons, we are rich!

He has forgiven us (v. 7b). The word *forgive* means "to carry away." This reminds us of the ritual on the Jewish day of Atonement, when the high priest sent the scapegoat into the wilderness (Lev. 16). First the priest killed one of the two goats and sprinkled its blood before God on the mercy seat. Then he confessed Israel's sins over the live goat, and had the goat taken into the wilderness to be lost. Christ died to carry away our sins so they might never again be seen (Ps. 103:12; John 1:29). No written accusation stands against us because our sins have been taken away! Sin made us poor, but grace makes us rich.

He has revealed God's will to us (vv. 8–10). This letter has much to say about God's plan for His people, a plan that was not fully understood even in Paul's day. The word *mystery* has nothing to do with things eerie. It means a "sacred secret, once hidden but now revealed to God's people." We believers are a part of God's "inner circle." We are able to share in the secret that God will one day unite everything in Christ. Ever since sin came into the world, things have been falling apart. First, man was separated from God (Gen. 3). Then man was separated from man, as Cain killed Abel (Gen. 4). People tried to maintain a kind of unity by building the Tower of Babel (Gen. 11), but God judged them and scattered them across the world.

God called Abraham and put a difference between the Jew and the Gentile, a difference that was maintained until Christ's death on the cross. Sin is tearing everything apart, but in Christ, God will gather everything together in the culmination of the ages. We are a part of this great eternal program.

He has made us an inheritance (vv. 11–12). The King James Version reads, "In whom also we have obtained an inheritance," but "in whom also we were made an inheritance" is also a possible translation. Both are true and the one includes the other. In Christ we have a wonderful inheritance (1 Peter 1:1–4), and in Christ we are an inheritance. We are valuable to Him. Think of the price God paid to purchase us and make us part of His inheritance! God the Son is the Father's love gift to us; and we are the Father's love gift to His Son. Read John 17 and note how many times Christ called us "those whom thou hast given me." The church is Christ's body (Eph. 1:22–23), building (Eph. 2:19–22), and bride (Eph. 5:22–23); Christ's future inheritance is wrapped up in His church. We are "joint-heirs with Christ" (Rom. 8:17), which means that He cannot claim His inheritance apart from us!

BLESSINGS FROM GOD THE HOLY SPIRIT (1:13–14)

We move now from eternity past (Eph. 1:4–6) and history past (Eph. 1:7–12), to the immediate experience of the Ephesian Christians. The Holy Spirit had worked in their lives, and they knew it.

He has sealed us (v. 13). The entire process of salvation is given in this verse, so we had better examine it carefully. It tells how the sinner becomes a saint. First, he hears the gospel of salvation. This is the good news that Christ died for our sins, was buried, and rose again (1 Cor. 15:1ff.). The Ephesians were Gentiles, and the gospel came "to the Jew first" (Rom. 1:16). But Paul, a Jew, brought the gospel to the Gentiles as he shared the Word of God with them.

The Ephesians "heard the gospel" and discovered it was for them—"your salvation" (Eph. 1:13). Even though the Bible teaches election, it also announces, "Go ye into all the world, and preach the gospel to every creature" (Mark 16:15). A soul winner does not discuss election with unsaved people, because it is a family secret that belongs to the saints. He simply announces the truth of the gospel and invites men to trust Christ, and the Holy Spirit does the rest. D. L. Moody used to pray, "Lord, save the elect—and then elect some more!" The same God who ordains the end, the salvation of souls, also ordains the means to the end, the preaching of the gospel in the power of the Spirit.

Having heard the Word, the Ephesians believed, and it is this faith that brought salvation (Eph. 2:8–9). This pattern follows what Paul wrote in Romans 10:13–15, so read that passage carefully. It is God's plan for evangelism. When the Ephesians believed, they were "sealed with the Spirit." "After that ye believed" should read *"when* ye believed." You receive the Spirit immediately on trusting Christ. This is not an experience subsequent to conversion. (Read Acts 10:34–48.)

What is the significance of this sealing of the Holy Spirit? For one thing, it speaks of a *finished transaction.* Even today, when important legal documents are processed, they are stamped with the official seal to signify the completion of the transaction. This sealing also implies *ownership:* God has put his seal on us because He has purchased us to be His own (1 Cor. 6:19–20). It also means *security and protection.* The Roman seal on the tomb of Jesus carried this meaning (Matt. 27:62–66). So, the believer belongs to God, and is safe and protected because he is a part of a finished transaction. According to John 14:16–17, the Holy Spirit abides with the believer forever. It is possible for us to grieve the Spirit and thereby lose the blessings of His ministry (Eph. 4:30). But He doesn't leave us.

Another use for the seal is as a mark of *authenticity.* Just as a signature on a letter attests to the genuineness of the document, so the presence of the Spirit proves the believer is genuine. "If any man have not the Spirit of Christ, he is none of his" (Rom. 8:9). It is not simply our lip profession, our religious activity, or our good works, but the witness of the Spirit that makes our profession authentic.

He has given us an earnest (v. 14). *Earnest* is a fascinating word! In Paul's day, it meant "the down payment to guarantee the final purchase of some commodity or piece of property." Even today you will hear a real estate agent talk about earnest money. The Holy Spirit is God's first installment to guarantee to His children that He will finish His work and eventually bring them to glory. The "redemption of the purchased possession" refers to the redemption of the body at the return of Christ (Rom. 8:18–23; 1 John 3:1–3). "Redemption" is experienced in three stages:

- We *have been redeemed* through faith in Jesus Christ (Eph. 1:7).
- We *are being redeemed* as the Spirit works in our lives to make us more like Christ (Rom. 8:1–4).
- We *shall be redeemed* when Christ returns and we become like Him.

But the word translated "earnest" also means "engagement ring." In Greece today you would find this word being used that way. But, after all, isn't an engagement ring an assurance—a guarantee—that the promises made will be kept? Our relationship to God through Christ is not simply a *commercial* one, but also a personal experience of love. He is the Bridegroom and His church is the bride. We know that He will come and claim His bride because He has given us His promise and His Spirit as the "engagement ring." What greater assurance could we want?

We have examined a number of basic Bible doctrines in this chapter, all on the theme of our riches in Christ. It would be profitable for us to review what these verses teach us.

1. *True riches come from God.* It is a source of great encouragement to

know that Father, Son, and Holy Spirit are all working on my behalf to make me rich. God not only gives us "richly all things to enjoy" (1 Tim. 6:17), but He gives us *eternal* riches without which all other wealth is valueless.

A distraught wife sought out a Christian marriage counselor and told her sad story of a marriage about to dissolve. "But we have so much!" she kept saying. "Look at this diamond ring on my finger. Why, it's worth thousands! We have an expensive mansion in an exclusive area. We have three cars, and even a cabin in the mountains. Why, we have everything money can buy!"

The counselor replied, "It's good to have the things money can buy provided you don't lose the things money can't buy. What good is an expensive house if there's no home? Or an expensive ring if there's no love?"

In Christ, you and I have "what money can't buy," and these spiritual riches open up to us all the wealth of God's vast creation. We enjoy the gifts because we know and love the Giver.

2. *All of these riches come by God's grace and for God's glory.* Did you notice that after each of the main sections in Ephesians 1:4–14, Paul added the purpose behind these gifts? Why has God the Father chosen us, adopted us, and accepted us? "To the praise of the glory of his grace" (Eph. 1:6). Why has the Son redeemed us, forgiven us, revealed God's will to us, and made us part of God's inheritance? "That we should be to the praise of his glory" (Eph. 1:12). Why has God the Spirit sealed us and become the guarantee of our future blessing? "Unto the praise of his glory" (Eph. 1:14).

We often have the idea that God saves sinners mainly because He pities them or wants to rescue them from eternal judgment, but God's main purpose is that He might be glorified. His creation reveals His wisdom and power, but His church reveals His love and grace. You cannot deserve or earn these spiritual riches; you can only receive them by grace, through faith.

3. *These riches are only the beginning!* There is always more spiritual wealth to claim from the Lord as we walk with Him. The Bible is our guidebook; the Holy Spirit is our Teacher. As we search the Word of God, we discover more and more of the riches we have in Christ. These riches were planned by the Father, purchased by the Son, and presented by the Spirit. There is really no need for us to live in poverty when all of God's wealth is at our disposal!

My friend was discussing money matters with his wife, and neither of them realized that their little son was listening. Finally the boy broke in with the suggestion, "Why don't you just write one of those pieces of paper?" Junior did not understand that it was necessary to have money in the bank to back up "those pieces of paper." But we never face that problem when it comes to our spiritual wealth.

A little devotional book by Charles Spurgeon is titled *A Checkbook on the Bank of Faith.* A promise from the Bible was given for each day of the year, along with a short devotional message. The author described each promise as being as good as money in the bank to anyone who would claim it by faith, as a person would write a check against his bank account. By faith we can claim God's promises and draw on His limitless wealth to meet every need we may face.

QUESTIONS FOR PERSONAL REFLECTION
OR GROUP DISCUSSION

1. What blessings have you received this past week?

2. Read Ephesians 1:4–14. How does it matter that God chose you before He created the world?

3. Why did God choose you for His blessings?

4. How did your spiritual adoption take place?

5. God chose you to be holy and blameless (v. 4). What does it mean to be holy and blameless? How can you possibly become that?

6. What is redemption? Why do you need it?

7. Do you live as if you are forgiven? Explain.

8. What is the inheritance that Paul mentions in Ephesians 1:14?

9. What blessings do we receive from God the Holy Spirit? How aware of them in your life are you?

10. How are all three persons of the Godhead involved in our salvation?

11. How do you think you should live in light of these riches you have received?

Chapter Three

READ THE BANKBOOK

(Ephesians 1:15–23)

On January 6, 1822, the wife of a poor German pastor had a son, never dreaming that he would one day achieve world renown and great wealth. When Heinrich Schliemann was seven years old, a picture of ancient Troy in flames captured his imagination. Contrary to what many people believed, Heinrich argued that Homer's great poems, the *Iliad* and the *Odyssey,* were based on historic facts and he set out to prove it. In 1873, he uncovered the ancient site of Troy, along with some fabulous treasure, which he smuggled out of the country, much to the anger of the Turkish government. Schliemann became a famous, wealthy man because he dared to believe an ancient record and act on his faith.

We discovered that we were "born rich" when we trusted Christ. But this is not enough, for we must grow in our understanding of our riches if we are ever going to use them to the glory of God. Too many Christians have never "read the bankbook" to find out the vast spiritual wealth that God has put to their account through Jesus Christ. They are like the late newspaper publisher, William Randolph Hearst, who invested a fortune collecting art treasures from around the world. One day Mr. Hearst found a description of some valuable items that he felt he must own, so he sent his agent abroad to find them. After months of searching, the agent reported that he had finally found the treasures. They were in Mr. Hearst's warehouse. Hearst had been searching frantically for treasures he already owned! Had he read the catalog of his treasures, he would have saved himself a great deal of money and trouble.

Paul desired the Ephesian Christians to understand what great wealth they had in Christ. Paul knew of their faith and love, and in this he rejoiced. The Christian life has two dimensions: faith toward God and love toward men, and you cannot separate the two. But Paul knew that faith and love were just the beginning. The Ephesians needed to know much more. This is why he prayed for them, and for us.

In the prison prayers of Paul (Eph. 1:15–23; 3:14–21; Phil. 1:9–11; Col. 1:9–12), we discover the blessings he wanted his converts to enjoy. In none of these prayers did Paul request material things. His emphasis was on spiritual perception and real Christian character. He did not ask God to give them what they did not have, but rather prayed that God would reveal to them what they already had.

Before we study Paul's four requests in this "prayer for enlightenment," we must notice two facts. First, enlightenment comes from the Holy Spirit. He is the "Spirit of wisdom and revelation" (Isa. 11:2; John 14:25–26; 16:12–14). With his natural mind, man cannot understand the things of God. He needs the Spirit to enlighten him (1 Cor. 2:9–16). The Holy Spirit reveals truth to us from the Word, and then gives us the wisdom to understand and apply it. He also gives us the power—the enablement—to practice the truth (Eph. 3:14–21).

Second, this enlightenment comes to the heart of the believer (Eph. 1:18 NIV). Literally this verse reads, "The eyes of your heart may be enlightened." We think of the heart as the emotional part of man, but in the Bible, the heart means the inner man, and includes the emotions, the mind, and the will. The inner man, the heart, has spiritual faculties that parallel the physical senses. The inner man can *see* (Ps. 119:18; John 3:3), *hear* (Matt. 13:9; Heb. 5:11), *taste* (Ps. 34:8; 1 Peter 2:3), *smell* (Phil. 4:18; 2 Cor. 2:14), and *touch* (Acts 17:27). This is what Jesus meant when He said of the people, "They seeing see not, and hearing they hear not" (Matt. 13:13). The inability to see and understand spiritual things is not the fault of the intelligence but of the heart. The eyes of the heart must be opened by the Spirit of God.

1. THAT THEY MIGHT KNOW GOD (1:17B)

This, of course, is the highest knowledge possible. The *atheist* claims there is no God for us to know, and the *agnostic* states that if there is a God we cannot know Him. But Paul has met God in the person of Jesus Christ, and he knows that a man really cannot understand much of anything else without a knowledge of God.

This willful ignorance of God led mankind into corruption and condemnation. In Romans 1:18ff., Paul described the stages in man's devolution: from willful ignorance of God to idolatry (substituting a lie for the truth) to immorality and indecency. Where does it begin? It begins with an unwillingness to know God as Creator, Sustainer, Governor, Savior, and Judge.

The believer must grow in his knowledge of God. To know God personally is salvation (John 17:3). To know Him increasingly is sanctification (Phil. 3:10). To know Him perfectly is glorification (1 Cor. 13:9–12). Since we are made in the image of God (Gen. 1:26–28), the better we know God, the better we know ourselves and each other. It is not enough to know God only as Savior. We must get to know Him as Father, Friend, Guide, and the better we know Him, the more satisfying our spiritual lives will be.

A believer said to me one day after a Bible lesson, "I'm sure glad I came! You gave me two good verses to use on my wicked neighbor!" Surely there are times when we use God's Word as a sword to defeat the enemy, but that is not the primary purpose behind the writing of the Bible. As the familiar hymn puts it,

> Beyond the sacred page
> I seek Thee, Lord.
> My spirit pants for Thee,
> O living Word.

2. THAT WE MIGHT KNOW GOD'S CALLING (1:18A)

The word *called* is an important word in the Christian's vocabulary. The word *church* is a combination of two Greek words that mean "called out." Paul never tired of testifying that God called him "by his grace" (Gal. 1:15), and he reminded Timothy that the believer has a "holy calling" (2 Tim. 1:9). We have been "called out of darkness into his marvelous light" (1 Peter 2:9), and have even been "called to glory" (1 Peter 5:10). God calls us by His grace and not because of any merit that we may possess.

Paul wanted us to understand the hope that is ours because of this calling (Eph. 4:4). Some callings offer no hope, but the calling we have in Christ assures us of a delightful future. Keep in mind that the word *hope* in the Bible does not mean "I hope so," like a child hoping for a doll or a bike at Christmas. The word carries with it "assurance for the future." The believer's hope is, of course, the return of Jesus Christ for His church (1 Thess. 4:13–18; 1 John 3:1–3). When we were lost, we were "without hope" (Eph. 2:12 NIV), but in Jesus Christ, we have a "living hope" (1 Peter 1:3 NIV) that encourages us day by day.

Dr. Kenneth Chafin, a well-known Baptist author, tells about the pastor and deacon who were visiting prospective members and drove up to a beautiful suburban home surrounded by a velvet lawn and gorgeous landscaping. Two expensive cars stood in the driveway, and through the picture window, the men saw their prospect, lounging in an easy chair and watching TV. The deacon turned to his pastor and said, "What kind of good news do we have for *him?*"

How prone we are to confuse prices and values. Ephesus was a wealthy city. It boasted the temple of Diana, one of the wonders of the ancient world. Today, Ephesus is an archeologist's paradise, but all of its wealth and splendor are gone. But the Christians who once lived there are today in heaven, enjoying the glory of God!

The hope that belongs to our calling should be a dynamic force in our lives, encouraging us to be pure (1 John 2:28—3:3), obedient (Heb. 13:17), and faithful (Luke 12:42–48). The fact that we shall one day see Christ and be like Him should motivate us to live like Christ today.

3. THAT WE MIGHT KNOW GOD'S RICHES (1:18B)

This phrase does not refer to our inheritance in Christ (Eph. 1:11), but His inheritance in us. This is an amazing truth—that God should look on us as a part of His great wealth! Just as a man's wealth brings glory to his name, so God will get glory from the church because of what He has invested in us. When Jesus Christ returns, we shall be "to the praise of the glory of his grace" (Eph. 1:6).

God deals with us on the basis of our future, not our past. He said to cowardly Gideon, "The LORD is with thee, thou mighty man of valor" (Judg. 6:12). Jesus said to Andrew's brother, "Thou art Simon … thou shalt be called Cephas [a stone]" (John 1:42).

Gideon did become a mighty man of valor, and Simon did become Peter, a rock. We Christians live in the future tense, our lives controlled by what we shall be when Christ returns. Because we are God's inheritance, we live to please and glorify Him.

This truth suggests to us that Christ will not enter into His promised glory until the church is there to share it with Him. He prayed for this before He died, and this prayer will be answered (John 17:24). Christ will be glorified in us (2 Thess. 1:10), and we will be glorified in Him (Col. 3:4). Knowing this should lead the believer into a life of dedication and devotion to the Lord.

4. THAT WE MIGHT KNOW GOD'S POWER (1:19–23)

By making us His inheritance, God has shown His love. By promising us a wonderful future, He has encouraged our hope. Paul offered something to challenge our faith: "the exceeding greatness of his power to us-ward who believe" (Eph. 1:19). So tremendous is this truth that Paul enlisted many different words from the Greek vocabulary to get his point across: *dunamis*—"power" as in dynamo and dynamite; *energeia*—"working" as in energy; *kratos*—"mighty"; *ischus*—"power." Ephesians 1:19 can be translated, "What is the surpassing greatness of His power toward us who believe, according to the operation of the might of His strength." He is talking about divine, dynamic, eternal energy, available to us!

After all, what good is it to have wealth if you are too weak to use it? Or if you are so afraid of robbers that you cannot really enjoy it? John D. Rockefeller was the world's first billionaire. It is said that for many years, he lived on crackers and milk because of stomach troubles caused by worrying about his wealth. He rarely had a good night's sleep, and guards stood constantly at his door. Wealthy—but miserable! When he began to share his wealth with others in great philanthropic endeavors, his health improved considerably and he lived to be an old man.

We Christians need power for several reasons. To begin with, by nature we are too weak to appreciate and appropriate this wealth, and to use it as it should be used. "The spirit indeed is willing, but the flesh is weak"

(Matt. 26:41). To turn this vast spiritual wealth over to a mere human being, living by human wisdom and strength, would be like handing an atomic bomb to a two-year-old. God's power enables us to use God's wealth.

But there is a second reason why we need God's power. There are enemies who want to rob us of our wealth (Eph. 1:21; 6:11–12). We could never defeat these spiritual foes in our own power, but we can through the Spirit's power. Paul wanted us to know the greatness of God's power so that we would not fail to use our wealth, and so that the enemy would not deprive us of our wealth.

The power is seen in the resurrection of Jesus Christ. In the Old Testament people measured God's power by His creation (Isa. 40:12–27) or by His miracle at the exodus of Israel from Egypt (Jer. 16:14). But today, we measure God's power by the miracle of Christ's resurrection. Much more was involved than merely raising Him from the dead, for Christ also ascended to heaven and sat down in the place of authority at the right hand of God. He is not only Savior; He is also Sovereign (Acts 2:25–36). No authority or power, human or in the spirit world, is greater than that of Jesus Christ, the exalted Son of God. He is "far above all," and no future enemy can overcome Him, because He has been exalted "far above all" powers.

But how does this apply to you and me today? In Ephesians 1:22–23, Paul explained the practical application. Because we are believers, we are in the church, which is Christ's body—and He is the Head. This means that there is a living connection between you and Christ. Physically speaking, the head controls the body and keeps the body functioning properly. Injure certain parts of the brain and you handicap or paralyze corresponding parts of the body. Christ is our spiritual Head. Through the Spirit, we are united to Him as the members of His body. This means that we share His resurrection, ascension, and exaltation. (Paul will amplify this later.) We too are seated in the heavenlies (Eph. 2:6), and all things are under our feet.

No wonder Paul wants us to know "the exceeding greatness of his power to us-ward"! Apart from this power, we cannot draw on our great wealth in Christ.

I recall going to the hospital with one of our church members to try to get her husband to sign a paper that would authorize her to draw on his private checking account so she could pay his bills. The man was so weak he could not sign the paper. She finally had to get witnesses to verify his "X" on the document. His weakness nearly deprived her of his wealth.

The power of the Holy Spirit, through the resurrected, ascended Christ, is available to all Christians—by faith. His power is to "us-ward who believe" (Eph. 1:19). It is grace that supplies the wealth, but it is faith that lays hold of the wealth. We are saved "by grace, through faith" (Eph. 2:8–9), and we live "by grace," through faith (1 Cor. 15:10).

In the four gospels, we see God's power at work in the ministry of Jesus Christ, but in the book of Acts, we see that same power at work in ordinary men and women, members of the body of Christ. What a transformation took place in Peter's life between the end of the Gospels and the beginning of Acts. What made the difference? The resurrection power of Jesus Christ (Acts 1:8).

The greatest power shortage today is not in our generators or our gas tanks. It is in our personal lives. Will Paul's prayer be answered in your life? Will you, starting today, begin to know by experience God—God's calling—God's riches—and God's power?

QUESTIONS FOR PERSONAL REFLECTION
OR GROUP DISCUSSION

1. Read Paul's prayer for the Ephesian believers in Ephesians 1:15–23. What motivated Paul to pray for them?

2. Paul prayed for his readers to know God better. What does knowing God involve? How well do you know Him?

3. What is hope? How is it related to your calling?

4. What does it look like for you to live as a person with hope rather than hopelessness?

5. How did God demonstrate His power to us?

6. Why do we need God's power?

7. Which is a greater temptation for you: to live as if you are powerless and no power is available, or to live as if you have plenty of power without relying on God? Explain.

8. How does Paul's prayer compare with how you typically pray?

9. Which of the things Paul prays for do you most need to pray for? Why that?

Chapter Four

GET OUT OF THE GRAVEYARD

(Ephesians 2:1–10)

Having described our spiritual *possessions* in Christ, Paul turned to a complementary truth: our spiritual *position* in Christ. First he explained what God has done for all sinners in general; then he explained what God did for the Gentiles in particular. The sinner who trusts Christ has been raised and seated on the throne (Eph. 2:1–10), and believing Jews and Gentiles have been reconciled and set into the temple (Eph. 2:11–22). What a miracle of God's grace! We are taken out of the great graveyard of sin and placed into the throne room of glory.

Perhaps the easiest way for us to approach this long paragraph is to see in it four specific works.

1. SIN'S WORK AGAINST US (2:1–3)

A publisher asked me for a full-length portrait that they could "blow up" and use as a life-size display at their convention booth to promote my tapes. A friend of mine took the picture, and it was a new experience for me. I had been accustomed to sitting for head-and-shoulder photographs, but standing for a full-length photo was something new. I had to watch my posture, the feet had to be placed just right, and the arms and hands—usually forgotten—had to be in just the right position. Fortunately, my photographer friend is an expert, and we managed to get a decent picture in a short time. In these three verses, Paul gave us a full-length picture of the terrible spiritual condition of the unsaved person. Note his characteristics.

He is dead (v. 1). Of course, this means spiritually dead; that is, he is unable to understand and appreciate spiritual things. He possesses no spiritual life, and he can do nothing of himself to please God. Just as a person physically dead does not respond to physical stimuli, so a person spiritually dead is unable to respond to spiritual things. A corpse does not hear the conversation going on in the funeral parlor. He has no appetite for food or drink; he feels no pain; he is dead. Just so with the inner man of the unsaved person. His spiritual faculties are not functioning, and they cannot function until God gives him life. The cause of this spiritual death is "trespasses and sins" (Eph. 2:1). "The wages of sin is death" (Rom. 6:23). In the Bible, *death* basically means "separation," not only physically, as the spirit separated from the body (James 2:26), but also spiritually, as the spirit separated from God (Isa. 59:2).

The unbeliever is not sick; he is dead! He does not need resuscitation; he needs resurrection. All lost sinners are dead, and the only difference between one sinner and another is the state of decay. The lost derelict on skid row may be more decayed outwardly than the unsaved society leader, but both are dead in sin—and one corpse cannot be more dead than another! This means that our world is one vast graveyard, filled with people who are dead while they live (1 Tim. 5:6).

He is disobedient (vv. 2–3a). This was the beginning of man's spiritual death—his disobedience to the will of God. God said, "In the day that thou eatest thereof thou shalt surely die" (Gen. 2:17). Satan said, "Ye shall not surely die" (Gen. 3:4), and because they believed this lie, the first man and woman sinned and experienced immediate spiritual death and ultimate physical death. Since that time, mankind has lived in disobedience to God. There are three forces that encourage man in his disobedience—the world, the Devil, and the flesh.

The world, or world-system, puts pressure on each person to try to get him to conform (Rom. 12:2). Jesus Christ was not "of this world" and neither are His people (John 8:23; 17:14). But the unsaved person, either consciously or unconsciously, is controlled by the values and attitudes of this world.

The Devil is "the spirit that now worketh in the children of disobedience." This does not mean that Satan is personally at work in the life of each unbeliever, since Satan as a created being is limited in space. Unlike God, who is omnipresent, Satan cannot be in all places at one time. But because of his demonic associates (Eph. 6:11–12) and his power over the world system (John 12:31), Satan influences the lives of all unbelievers, and also seeks to influence believers. He wants to make people "children of disobedience" (Eph. 2:2; 5:6). He himself was disobedient to God, so he wants others to disobey Him too.

One of Satan's chief tools for getting people to disobey God is lies. He is a liar (John 8:44), and it was his lie at the beginning of human history, "Ye shall not surely die," that plunged the human race into sin. The unsaved multitudes in today's world system disobey God because they believe the lies of Satan. When a person believes and practices a lie, he becomes a child of disobedience.

The flesh is the third force that encourages the unbeliever to disobey God. By *the flesh* Paul does not mean the body, because of itself, the body is not sinful. *The flesh* refers to that fallen nature that we were born with, that wants to control the body and the mind and make us disobey God. An evangelist friend of mine once announced as his topic, "Why Your

Dog Does What It Does," and, of course, many dog lovers came out to hear him. What he had to say was obvious, but too often overlooked: "A dog behaves like a dog because he has a dog's nature." If somehow you could transplant into the dog the nature of the cat, his behavior would change radically. Why does a sinner behave like a sinner? Because he has the nature of a sinner (Ps. 51:5; 58:3). This sinful nature the Bible calls "the flesh."

Is it any wonder that the unsaved person is disobedient to God? He is controlled by the world, the flesh, and the Devil, the three great enemies of God! And he cannot change his own nature or, of himself, overcome the world and the Devil. He needs outside help, and that help can come only from God.

He is depraved (v. 3b). The lost sinner lives to please the "desires of the flesh and the wishes of the mind" (literal translation). His actions are sinful because his appetites are sinful. When you apply the word *depraved* to the unsaved person, you are not saying that he *only* does evil, or that he is incapable of doing good. You are simply saying that he is incapable of doing anything to merit salvation or meet the high standards of God's holiness. Jesus said that lost sinners do good to each other (Luke 6:33) and to their children (Luke 11:13), but they cannot do anything spiritually good to please God. The people on Malta who kindly assisted Paul and his friends after the shipwreck certainly did good works, but they still needed to be saved (Acts 28:1–2).

He is doomed (v. 3c). By nature, children of wrath! By deed, children of disobedience! The unsaved person is condemned already (John 3:18). The sentence has been passed, but God in His mercy is staying the execution of the sentence (2 Peter 3:8–10). Man cannot save himself, but God in His grace steps in to make salvation possible. "But God!"—what a difference those two words make! This leads to the second work.

2. GOD'S WORK FOR US (2:4–9)

The focus of attention now is on God, not on sinful man. "Salvation is of the LORD" (Jonah 2:9). We are reminded of four activities that God performed on behalf of sinners to save them from the consequences of their sins.

He loved us (v. 4). By nature, "God is love" (1 John 4:8). But God would love even if there were no sinners, because love is a part of His very being. Theologians call love one of God's attributes. But God has two kinds of attributes: those that He possesses of Himself (intrinsic attributes, such as life, love, holiness) and those by which He relates to His creation, especially to man (relative attributes). For example, by nature God is *truth,* but when He relates to man, God's truth becomes *faithfulness. God* is by nature *holy,* and when He relates that holiness to man, it becomes *justice.*

Love is one of God's intrinsic attributes, but when this love is related to sinners, it becomes *grace* and *mercy.* God is "rich in mercy" (Eph. 2:4) and in "grace" (Eph. 2:7), and these riches make it possible for sinners to be saved. It comes as a shock to some people when they discover that we are not saved "by God's love," but by God's mercy and grace. In His mercy, He does not give us what we do deserve, and in His grace He gives us what we do not deserve. And all of this is made possible because of the death of Jesus Christ on the cross. It was at Calvary that God displayed His hatred for sin and His love for sinners (Rom. 5:8; John 3:16).

He quickened us (v. 5). This means He made us alive, even when we were dead in sins. He accomplished this spiritual resurrection by the power of the Spirit, using the Word. In the four gospels, it is recorded that Jesus raised three people from the dead: the widow's son (Luke 7:11–17), Jairus's daughter (Luke 8:49–56), and Lazarus (John 11:41–46). In each case, He spoke the Word and this gave life. "The Word of God is quick [living], and powerful" (Heb. 4:12). These three physical resurrections are pictures of the spiritual resurrection that comes to the sinner when he hears the Word and believes (John 5:24).

But our spiritual resurrection is much greater because it puts us in union with Christ: God "made us alive together with Christ." As members of His body we are united to Him (Eph. 1:22–23), so that we share His resurrection life and power (Eph. 1:19–20).

He exalted us (v. 6). We are not raised from the dead and left in the graveyard. Because we are united to Christ, we have been exalted with Him, and we are sharing His throne in the heavenlies. Our physical position may be on earth, but our spiritual position is "in heavenly places in Christ Jesus." Like Lazarus, we have been called from the grave to sit with Christ and enjoy His fellowship (John 12:1–2).

He keeps us (vv. 7–9). God's purpose in our redemption is not simply to rescue us from hell, as great a work as that is. His ultimate purpose in our salvation is that for all eternity the church might glorify God's grace (Eph. 1:6, 12, 14). So, if God has an eternal purpose for us to fulfill, He will keep us for all eternity. Since we have not been saved by our good works, we cannot be lost by our bad works. Grace means salvation completely apart from any merit or works on our part. Grace means that God does it all for Jesus' sake! Our salvation is the gift of God. (The word *that* in Eph. 2:8, in the Greek, is neuter; while *faith* is feminine. Therefore *that* cannot refer to *faith*. It refers to the whole experience of salvation, including faith.) Salvation is a gift, not a reward.

Salvation cannot be "of works" because the work of salvation has already been completed on the cross. This is the work that God does *for* us, and it is a finished work (John 17:1–4; 19:30). We can add nothing to it (Heb. 10:1–14); we dare take nothing from it. When Jesus died, the veil of the temple was torn in two, from the top to the bottom, signifying that the way to God was now open. There is no more need for earthly sacrifices. One sacrifice—the Lamb of God—has finished the great work of salvation. God did it all, and He did it by His grace.

Sin worked against us and God worked for us, but the great work of conversion is but the beginning.

3. GOD'S WORK IN US (2:10A)

"For we are his workmanship created in Christ Jesus." The Greek word translated "workmanship" is *poiema,* from which we derive our English word *poem.* It means "that which is made, a manufactured product." In other words, our conversion is not the end; it is the beginning. We are a part of God's "new creation" (2 Cor. 5:17), and God continues to work in us to make us what He wants us to be. His purpose is to make us more like Christ (Rom. 8:29).

But how does God work in us? Through His Holy Spirit, "both to will and to do of his good pleasure" (Phil. 2:13). Christ finished His work of redemption on the cross, but He arose from the dead and returned to heaven. There He carries on His unfinished work of perfecting His church (Eph. 4:7–16; Heb. 13:20–21). Christ is equipping us for our walk and our work here on earth. To do this, He uses three special tools: the Word of God (1 Thess. 2:13), prayer (Eph. 3:20–21), and suffering (1 Peter 4:11–14). As we read God's Word, understand it, meditate on it, and feed on it, the Word goes to work in our lives to cleanse us and nourish us. As we pray, God's Spirit works in us to release power. And as we suffer, the Spirit of God ministers to us. Suffering drives us back to the Word and prayer, and the cycle is repeated.

Too many Christians think that conversion is the only important experience, and that nothing follows. But this is wrong. We can use the resurrection of Lazarus as an example. After Jesus raised Lazarus from the dead, He said, "Loose him, and let him go" (John 11:44). In other words, "This man is now alive. Get him out of the graveclothes!" Paul had this concept in mind in Ephesians 4:22–24 when he wrote, "That ye put off concerning the former conversation [behavior] the old man, which is corrupt … and that ye put on the new man, which after God is created in righteousness and true holiness." Colossians 3:1 has the same message: "[Since] ye then be risen with Christ, seek those things which are above."

The same resurrection power that saved you and took you out of the graveyard of sin can daily help you live for Christ and glorify Him. At great expense to Himself, God worked for us on the cross. And today, on the basis of that price paid at Calvary, He is working in us to conform us to Christ. God cannot work in us unless He has first worked for us, and we have trusted His Son. Also, He cannot work through us unless He works in us. This is why it is important for you to spend time daily in the Word and prayer, and to yield to Christ during times of suffering. For it is through the Word, prayer, and suffering that God works in you.

The Bible shows many examples of this principle. God spent forty years working in Moses before He could work through him. At the beginning of his ministry, Moses was impetuous and depended on his own strength. He killed an Egyptian and had to flee Egypt, hardly a successful way to start a ministry. But during those forty years as a humble shepherd in the desert, Moses experienced God's working in his life, a working that prepared him for forty more years of magnificent service.

There are other examples. Joseph suffered for thirteen years before God put him on the throne of Egypt, second to Pharaoh. David was anointed king when he was a youth, but he did not gain the throne until he had suffered many years as an exile. Even the apostle Paul spent three years in Arabia after his conversion, no doubt experiencing God's deeper work to prepare him for his ministry. God has to work in us before He can work through us; and this leads to the fourth work in our passage.

4. GOD'S WORK THROUGH US (2:10B)

We are "created in Christ Jesus unto good works." We are not saved by good works, but saved unto good works. The famous theologian John Calvin wrote, "It is faith alone that justifies, but faith that justifies can never be alone." We are not saved by faith plus good works, but by a faith that works. The basic Scripture on this theme is James 2, where the writer points out that saving faith always results in a changed life. It is not enough to say that we have faith; we must demonstrate this faith by our works.

The Bible speaks of many different kinds of works. There are "the works of the law," which cannot save (Gal. 2:16; 3:11). There are also "the works of the flesh," which are listed in Galatians 5:19–21. Paul spoke of "works of darkness" (Rom. 13:12; Eph. 5:11). The "dead works" in Hebrews 6:1 seem to be "works that lead to death," since "the wages of sin is death" (Rom. 6:23). The "works of righteousness" in Titus 3:5 refer to religious works, or other good deeds, that sinners try to practice as a means of salvation. Isaiah declared that "all our righteousnesses are as filthy rags" (Isa. 64:6). If our righteousnesses are filthy, what must our sins look like!

The "works" Paul wrote about in Ephesians 2:10 have two special characteristics. First, they are "good" works, in contrast to "works of darkness" and "wicked works." If you contrast Ephesians 2:10 with Ephesians 2:2 you will see that the unbeliever has Satan working in him, and therefore his works are not good. But the believer has God working in him, and therefore his works are good. His works are not good because he himself is good, but because he has a new nature from God, and because the Holy Spirit works in him and through him to produce these good works.

It is too bad that many believers minimize the place of good works in the Christian life. Because we are not saved by good works, they have the idea that good works are evil; and this is a mistake. "Let your light so shine before men, that they may see your good works, and glorify your Father which is in heaven" (Matt. 5:16). We do not perform good works to glorify ourselves, but to glorify God. Paul desired that Christ would be magnified in his body, even if it meant death (Phil. 1:20–21). We should "abound to every good work" (2 Cor. 9:8), and be "fruitful in every good work" (Col. 1:10). One result of a knowledge of the Bible is that the believer is "thoroughly equipped for every good work" (2 Tim. 3:17 NIV). As believers, we are to be "zealous of good works" (Titus 2:14). Our good works are actually "spiritual sacrifices" that we offer to God (Heb. 13:16).

It is important to note that we do not manufacture these good works. They are the results of the work of God in our hearts. "It is God which worketh in you both to will and to do of his good pleasure" (Phil. 2:13). The secret of Paul's good works was "the grace of God" (1 Cor. 15:10). Our good works are evidence that we have been born again. "Not every one that saith unto me, Lord, Lord, shall enter into the kingdom of heaven; but he that doeth the will of my Father which is in heaven" (Matt. 7:21). Our good works are also testimonies to the lost (1 Peter 2:12). They win us the right to be heard.

A pastor friend told about a Christian woman who often visited a retirement home near her house. One day she noticed a lonely man sitting, staring at his dinner tray. In a kindly manner she asked, "Is something wrong?"

"Is something wrong!" replied the man in a heavy accent. "Yes, something is wrong! I am a Jew, and I cannot eat this food!"

"What would you like to have?" she asked.

"I would like a bowl of hot soup!"

She went home and prepared the soup and, after getting permission from the office, took it to the man. In succeeding weeks, she often visited him and brought him the kind of food he enjoyed, and eventually she led him to faith in Christ. Yes, preparing soup can be a spiritual sacrifice, a good work to the glory of God.

But these works are not only good; they are also "prepared." "Good works which God hath before ordained [prepared] that we should walk in them" (Eph. 2:10). The only other time this word is used in the New Testament is in Romans 9:23: "vessels of mercy, which he had afore prepared unto glory." The unbeliever walks "according to the course of this world" (Eph. 2:2), but the believer walks in the good works God has prepared for him.

This is an amazing statement. It means that God has a plan for our lives and that we should walk in His will and fulfill His plan. Paul is not talking about "kismet"—an impersonal fate that controls your life no matter what you may do. He is talking about the gracious plan of a loving heavenly Father, who wills the very best for us. The will of God comes from the heart of God. "The counsel of the LORD standeth for ever, the thoughts of his heart to all generations" (Ps. 33:11). We discover God's exciting will for our lives as the Spirit reveals it to us from the Word (1 Cor. 2:9–13).

It would be helpful to close this chapter with a personal inventory. Which of these four works are you experiencing? Is sin working against you because you have not yet trusted Christ? Then trust Him now! Have you experienced His work *for* you—*in* you—*through* you?

Are you wearing the "graveclothes" or the "grace-clothes"? Are you enjoying the liberty you have in Christ, or are you still bound by the habits of the old life in the graveyard of sin? As a Christian, you have been raised and seated on the throne. Practice your position in Christ! He has worked *for* you; now let Him work *in* you and *through* you, that He might give you an exciting, creative life to the glory of God.

QUESTIONS FOR PERSONAL REFLECTION
OR GROUP DISCUSSION

1. Read Ephesians 2:1–10. What does Paul mean when he says his readers were dead?

2. How is the flesh different from the body? Why does this distinction matter?

3. There are lots of unbelievers who live moral lives. How can a person live to satisfy the cravings of the flesh and still live a basically moral life?

4. How do you respond to the idea that basically decent people are disobedient and influenced by the Devil?

5. Are you more alive than the unbelievers you know? If so, how?

6. How does God make dead people come alive?

7. Paul says you are seated with Christ in the heavenly realm. What does he mean? How can that be true of you while you still live on earth?

8. What is the relationship between good works and salvation?

9. What is the significance of the word *workmanship* in verse 10? How would thinking of yourself as God's workmanship affect the way you conduct your life?

10. How have you seen God working in you lately?

11. What good work is God giving you to do, with His power, this week?

Chapter Five

THE GREAT PEACE MISSION

(Ephesians 2:11–22)

Peace in our time! Peace with honor!" Some of us still remember those words of British Prime Minister Sir Neville Chamberlain when he returned from conferences in Germany in September 1938. He was sure that he had stopped Adolf Hitler. Yet one year later, Hitler invaded Poland, and on September 3, 1939, Great Britain declared war on Germany. Chamberlain's great peace mission had failed.

It seems that most peace missions fail. I read somewhere that from 1500 BC to AD 850 there were 7,500 "eternal covenants" agreed on among various nations with the hope of bringing peace, but that no covenant lasted longer than two years. The only "eternal covenant" that has lasted—and that will last—is the one made by the eternal God, sealed by the blood of Jesus Christ. It is Christ's peace mission that Paul explained in this section, and three very important words summarize this great work: separation, reconciliation, and unification.

1. SEPARATION: WHAT THE GENTILES WERE (2:11–12)

In the first ten verses of Ephesians 2, Paul discussed the salvation of sinners in general, but now he turned to the work of Christ for Gentiles in particular. Most of the converts in the Ephesian church were Gentiles, and they knew that much of God's program in the Old Testament involved the Jews. For centuries, the "circumcision" (Jews) had looked down on the "uncircumcision" (Gentiles) with an attitude that God had never intended them to display. The fact that a Jew had received the physical mark of the covenant was no proof he was a man of faith (Rom. 2:25–29; Gal. 5:6; 6:15). Those who have trusted Christ have received a spiritual circumcision "made without hands" (Col. 2:11).

But since the hour that God called Abraham, God made a difference between Jews and Gentiles. He made this difference, not that the Jews might boast, but that they might be a blessing and a help to the Gentiles. God set them apart that He might use them to be a channel of His revelation and goodness to the heathen nations. Sad to say, Israel kept this difference nationally and ritually, but not morally. Israel became like the lost nations around her. For this reason, God often had to discipline the Jews because they would not maintain their spiritual separation and minister to the nations in the name of the true God.

The one word that best describes the Gentiles is *without*. They were "outside" in several respects.

Without Christ. The Ephesians worshipped the goddess Diana and, before the coming of the gospel, knew nothing about Christ. Those who claim that pagan religions are just as acceptable to God as the Christian faith will have a problem here, for Paul cites the Ephesians' Christless state as a definite tragedy. But then, keep in mind that every unsaved person, Jew or Gentile, is "outside Christ," and that means condemnation.

Without citizenship. God called the Jews and built them into a nation. He gave them His laws and His blessings. A Gentile could enter the nation as a proselyte, but he was not born into that very special nation. Israel was God's nation, in a way that was not true of any Gentile nation.

Without covenants. While the blessing of the Gentiles is included in God's covenant with Abraham (Gen. 12:1–3), God did not make any covenants with the Gentile nations. The Gentiles were "aliens" and "strangers"—and the Jews never let them forget it. Many of the Pharisees would pray daily, "O God, I give thanks that I am a Jew, not a Gentile."

Without hope. Historians tell us that a great cloud of hopelessness covered the ancient world. Philosophies were empty; traditions were disappearing; religions were powerless to help men face either life or death. People longed to pierce the veil and get some message of hope from the other side, but there was none (1 Thess. 4:13–18).

Without God. The heathen had gods aplenty, as Paul discovered in Athens (Acts 17:16–23). Someone in that day said that it was easier to find a god than a man in Athens. "There be gods many, and lords many," wrote Paul (1 Cor. 8:5). But the pagan, no matter how religious or moral he might have been, did not know the true God. The writer of Psalm 115 contrasted the true God with the idols of the heathen.

It is worth noting that the spiritual plight of the Gentiles was caused not by God but by their own willful sin. Paul said the Gentiles knew the true God but deliberately refused to honor Him (Rom. 1:18–23). Religious history is not a record of man starting with many gods (idolatry) and gradually discovering the one true God.

Rather, it is the sad story of man knowing the truth about God and deliberately turning away from it! It is a story of devolution, not evolution! The first eleven chapters of Genesis give the story of the decline of the Gentiles, and from Genesis 12 on (the call of Abraham), it is the story of the Jews. God separated the Jews from the Gentiles that He might be able to save the Gentiles also. "Salvation is of the Jews" (John 4:22).

God called the Jews, beginning with Abraham, that through them He might reveal Himself as the one true God. With the Jews He deposited His

Word, and through the Jews He gave the world the Savior (Rom. 9:1–5). Israel was to be a light to the Gentiles that they too might be saved. But sad to say, Israel became like the Gentiles, and the light burned but dimly. This fact is a warning to the church today. When the church is least like the world, it does the most for the world.

2. RECONCILIATION: WHAT GOD DID FOR THE GENTILES (2:13–18)

The "but now" in Ephesians 2:13 parallels the "but God" in Ephesians 2:4. Both speak of the gracious intervention of God on behalf of lost sinners. "Enmity" is the key word in this section (Eph. 2:15–16), and you will note that it is a twofold enmity: between Jews and Gentiles (Eph. 2:13–15) and between sinners and God (Eph. 2:16–18). Paul described here the greatest peace mission in history: Jesus Christ not only reconciled Jews and Gentiles, but He reconciled both to Himself in the one body, the church.

The word *reconcile* means "to bring together again." A distraught husband wants to be reconciled to his wife who has left him; a worried mother longs to be reconciled to a wayward daughter; and the lost sinner needs to be reconciled to God. Sin is the great separator in this world. It has been dividing people since the very beginning of human history. When Adam and Eve sinned, they were separated from God. Before long, their sons were separated from each other and Cain killed Abel. The earth was filled with violence (Gen. 6:5–13), and the only remedy seemed to be judgment. But even after the flood, men sinned against God and each other, and even tried to build their own unity without God's help. The result was another judgment that scattered the nations and confused the tongues. It was then that God called Abraham, and through the nation of Israel, Jesus Christ came to the world. It was His work on the cross that abolished the enmity between Jew and Gentile and between sinners and God.

The enmity between Jews and Gentiles (vv. 13–15). God had put a difference between Jews and Gentiles so that His purposes in salvation might be accomplished. But once those purposes were accomplished, there was no more difference. In fact, it was His purpose that these differences be erased forever, and they are erased through the work of Christ in reconciliation.

It was this lesson that was so difficult for the early church to understand. For centuries, the Jews had been different from the Gentiles—in religion, dress, diet, and laws. Until Peter was sent to the Gentiles (Acts 10), the church had no problems. But with the salvation of the Gentiles on the same terms as the Jews, problems began to develop. The Jewish Christians reprimanded Peter for going to the Gentiles and eating with them (Acts 11), and representatives of the churches gathered for an important conference on the place of the Gentiles in the church (Acts 15). Must a Gentile become a Jew to become a Christian? Their conclusion was, "No! Jews and Gentiles are saved the same way—by faith in Jesus Christ." The enmity was gone!

The cause of that enmity was the law, because the law made a definite distinction between Jews and Gentiles. The dietary laws reminded the Jews that God had put a difference between the clean and unclean (Lev. 11:44–47). But the Gentiles did not obey these laws; therefore they were unclean. Ezekiel the prophet reminded the priests that their task was to teach the Jews "the difference between the holy and the profane" (Ezek. 44:23). The divine ordinances given by God to Israel stood as a wall between the Jews and the other nations. In fact, there was a wall in the Jewish temple, separating the court of the Gentiles from the rest of the temple areas. Archeologists have discovered the inscription from Herod's temple, and it reads like this:

> No foreigner may enter within the barricade which surrounds
> the sanctuary and enclosure. Anyone who is caught doing so will
> have himself to blame for his ensuing death.

It was this wall that the Jews thought Paul and his Gentile friends crossed when the Jews attacked him in the temple and threatened to kill him (Acts 21:28–31).

In order for Jews and Gentiles to be reconciled, this wall had to be destroyed, and this Jesus did on the cross. The cost of destroying the enmity was the blood of Christ. When He died, the veil in the temple was literally torn in two, and the wall of separation (figuratively) was torn down. By fulfilling the demands of the law in His righteous life, and by bearing the curse of the law in His sacrificial death (Gal. 3:10–13), Jesus removed the legal barrier that separated Jew from Gentile. For centuries, there was a difference between them. But today, "there is no difference between the Jew and the Greek: for the same Lord over all is rich unto all that call upon him. For whosoever shall call upon the name of the Lord shall be saved" (Rom. 10:12–13).

In Jesus Christ, Jew and Gentile become one. "He is our peace" (Eph. 2:14). Through Christ, the far-off Gentile is made "nigh" (Eph. 2:13, 17), and both Jew and Gentile are made one. The consequences of Christ's work are, then, the destroying of the enmity by the abolishing of the law, and the creating of a new *man*—the church, the body of Christ. The word *abolish* simply means "to nullify." The law no longer holds sway over either Jew or Gentile, since in Christ believers are not under law but under grace. The righteousness of the law, revealing God's holiness, is still God's standard. But this is fulfilled in the believer by the Holy Spirit (Rom. 8:1–4). It took the early church a long time to get accustomed to "there is no difference!" In fact, some religious groups have not learned the lesson yet, for they are trying to get Christians back under law (Gal. 4:8–11; 5:1; Col. 2:13–23).

Christ "is our peace" (Eph. 2:14) and He made "peace" (Eph. 2:15). That verb *to make* in Ephesians 2:15 means "to create." The church, the body of Christ, is God's new creation (2 Cor. 5:15). Everything in the old creation is falling apart because of sin, but in the new creation there is unity because of righteousness. "There is neither Jew nor Greek, there is neither bond nor free, there is neither male nor female: for ye are all one in Christ Jesus" (Gal. 3:28). You may contrast the old position of the Gentiles with their new position and see how wonderfully Christ worked on their behalf on the cross:

Old Position	*New Position*
"without Christ"	"in Christ" (Eph. 2:13)
"aliens"	"a holy nation" (1 Peter 2:9)
"strangers"	"no more strangers" (Eph. 2:19)
"no hope"	"called in one hope" (Eph. 4:4)
"without God" (Eph. 2:12)	"The God and Father of our Lord Jesus Christ" (Eph. 1:3)

The enmity between sinners and God (vv. 16–18). Not only did the Gentiles need to be reconciled to the Jews, but both the Jews and the Gentiles needed to be reconciled to God! This was the conclusion the apostles came to at the Jerusalem Conference recorded in Acts 15. Peter said that God "put no difference between us [Jews] and them [Gentiles], purifying their hearts by faith.… But we believe that through the grace of the LORD Jesus Christ we shall be saved, even as they" (Acts 15:9, 11). It was not a question of the Gentile becoming a Jew to become a Christian, but the Jew admitting he was a sinner like the Gentile. "For there is no difference: For all have sinned and come short of the glory of God" (Rom. 3:22–23). The same law that separated Gentile and Jew also separated men and God, and Christ bore the curse of the law.

A man stopped in my office one day and said he wanted to get help. "My wife and I need a re-cancellation!" he blurted out. I knew he meant "reconciliation." But in one sense, "re-cancellation" was the right word.

They had sinned against each other (and the Lord), and there could be no harmony until those sins were canceled. A God of love wants to reconcile the sinner to Himself, but a God of holiness must see to it that sin is judged. God solved the problem by sending His Son to be the sacrifice for our sins, thereby revealing His love and meeting the demands of His righteousness. It was truly a "re-cancellation" (see Col. 2:13–14).

Jesus Christ "is our peace" (Eph. 2:14). He "made peace" (Eph. 2:15), and He "preached peace" (Eph. 2:17). As the Judge, He could have come to declare war. But in His grace, He came with the message of peace (Luke 2:8–14; 4:16–19). Jew and Gentile are at peace with each other in Christ, and both have open access to God (Rom. 5:1–2). This reminds us of the rent veil at the time of Christ's death (Matt. 27:50–51; Heb. 10:14–25). Reconciliation is complete!

3. Unification: What Jews and Gentiles Are in Christ (2:19–22)

Paul repeated the word "one" to emphasize the unifying work of Christ: "made both one" (Eph. 2:14); "one new man" (Eph. 2:15); "one body" (Eph. 2:16); "one Spirit" (Eph. 2:18). All spiritual distance and division have been overcome by Christ. In the closing verses of this chapter, Paul gave three pictures that illustrate the unity of believing Jews and Gentiles in the church.

One nation (v. 19a). Israel was God's chosen nation, but they rejected their Redeemer and suffered the consequences. The kingdom was taken from them and given to "a nation bringing forth the fruits thereof" (Matt. 21:43). This "new nation" is the church, "a chosen generation … a holy nation, a peculiar people" (Ex. 19:6; 1 Peter 2:9). In the Old Testament, the nations were reckoned by their descent from Shem, Ham, or Japheth (Gen. 10). In the book of Acts, we see these three families united in

Christ. In Acts 8, a descendant of Ham is saved, the Ethiopian treasurer; in Acts 9, a descendant of Shem, Saul of Tarsus, who became Paul the apostle; and in Acts 10, the descendants of Japheth, the Gentiles in the household of the Roman soldier, Cornelius. Sin has divided mankind, but Christ unites by His Spirit. All believers, regardless of national background, belong to that "holy nation" with citizenship in heaven (Phil. 3:20–21).

One family (v. 19b). Through faith in Christ, we enter into God's family, and God becomes our Father. This wonderful family of God is found in two places, "in heaven and earth" (Eph. 3:15). Living believers are on earth; believers who have died are in heaven. None of God's children are "under the earth" (Phil. 2:10) or in any other place in the universe. We are all brothers and sisters in the one family, no matter what racial, national, or physical distinctions we may possess.

One temple (vv. 20–22). In the book of Genesis, God "walked" with His people (Gen. 5:22, 24; 6:9), but in Exodus, He decided to "dwell" with His people (Ex. 25:8). God dwelt in the tabernacle (Ex. 40:34–38) until Israel's sins caused "the glory to depart" (1 Sam. 4). Then God dwelt in the temple (1 Kings 8:1–11), but, alas, again Israel sinned and the glory departed (Ezek. 10:18–19). God's next dwelling place was the body of Christ (John 1:14), which men took and nailed to a cross. Today, through His Spirit, God dwells in the church, the temple of God. God does not dwell in man-made temples, including church buildings (Acts 7:48–50). He dwells in the hearts of those who have trusted Christ (1 Cor. 6:19–20), and in the church collectively (Eph. 2:20–22).

The foundation for this church was laid by the apostles and New Testament prophets. Jesus Christ is the Foundation (1 Cor. 3:11) and the Chief Cornerstone (Ps. 118:22; Isa. 8:14). The cornerstone binds the structure together; Jesus Christ has united Jews and Gentiles in the church. This reference to the temple would be meaningful to both the Jews and the Gentiles in the Ephesian church: The Jews would think of Herod's temple in Jerusalem, and the Gentiles would think of the great temple of Diana. Both temples were destined to be destroyed, but the temple Christ is building will last forever. "I will build my church" (Matt. 16:18). The Holy Spirit builds this temple by taking dead stones out of the pit of sin (Ps. 40:2), giving them life, and setting them lovingly into the temple of God (1 Peter 2:5). This temple is "fitly framed together" as the body of Christ (Eph. 2:21; 4:16), so that every part accomplishes the purpose God has in mind.

As you look back over this chapter, you cannot help but praise God for what He, in His grace, has done for sinners. Through Christ, He has raised us from the dead and seated us on the throne. He has reconciled us and set us into His temple. Neither spiritual *death* nor spiritual *distance* can defeat the grace of God! But He has not only saved us individually, He has also made us a part of His church collectively. What a tremendous privilege it is to be a part of God's eternal program!

This leads to two practical applications as we close this study.

First, have you personally experienced the grace of God? Are you spiritually dead? Are you distant from God? Or have you trusted Christ and received that eternal life that only He can give? If you are not sure of your spiritual position, I urge you to turn to Christ by faith and trust Him. Like the nation of Israel, you may have been given many spiritual privileges, only to reject the God who gave them. Or, like the Gentiles, you may have turned away from God and lived deliberately in sin and disobedience. In either case, "there is no difference: For all have sinned, and come short of the glory of God" (Rom. 3:22–23). Call on Christ— He will save you.

Second, if you are a true believer in Christ, are you helping others to trust Him? You have been raised from the dead—do you "walk in newness of life" (Rom. 6:4)? Do you share this good news of eternal life with others? You are no longer at enmity with God, but are you spreading the good news of "peace with God" with those who are still fighting Him?

Jesus Christ died to make reconciliation possible. You and I must live to make the message of reconciliation personal. God has "given to us the ministry of reconciliation" (2 Cor. 5:18). We are His ambassadors of peace (2 Cor. 5:20). Our feet should be shod "with the preparation of the gospel of peace" (Eph. 6:15). "Blessed are the peacemakers, for they shall be called the children of God" (Matt. 5:9).

A missionary was preaching in the village market, and some of the people were laughing at him because he was not a very handsome man. He took it for a time, and then he said to the crowd, "It is true that I do not have beautiful hair, for I am almost bald. Nor do I have beautiful teeth, for they are really not mine; they were made by the dentist. I do not have a beautiful face, nor can I afford to wear beautiful clothes. But this I know: I have beautiful feet!" And he quoted the verse from Isaiah: "How beautiful upon the mountains are the feet of him that bringeth good tidings, that publisheth peace" (Isa. 52:7). Do you have beautiful feet?

QUESTIONS FOR PERSONAL REFLECTION
OR GROUP DISCUSSION

1. What do people today mean by the word *peace*?

2. Are you a Jew or a Gentile? How does that affect the way you respond to Ephesians 2:11–22?

3. Without Christ, Paul says the Gentiles are also without citizenship, without a covenant, without hope, and without God. Is this true of unbelievers you know? If so, how?

4. What does it mean to be reconciled to another person?

5. Why is reconciliation needed between man and God?

6. Why is reconciliation between Jews and Gentiles significant?

7. How does this reconciliation affect your daily life?

8. How does God's peace contrast with the way people refer to "peace" today?

9. How aware are you of being an insider, a person who fully belongs and has been brought near? Why is that?

10. What are you doing to help people be reconciled to God?

Chapter Six

I KNOW A SECRET

(Ephesians 3:1–13)

I was once a character witness at a child-custody trial. I was grateful that the case was being tried at a small rural county seat rather than in a big city, because it was my first experience on the witness stand. I have since learned that the location of the court makes little difference. All trials can be difficult and it is no fun to be a witness at any.

The prosecutor's first question caught me unawares: "Reverend, do you think that a man who has been in prison is fit to raise a child?"

I was supposed to answer yes or no, so the reply I gave did not make the judge too happy. "Well," I said slowly, stalling for time, "I guess it depends on the man. Some very famous people have been in jail and have made the world a better place because of their experiences—John Bunyan, for example, and the great apostle Paul." I could have given other examples from the Bible, but I detected that my answer was not acceptable to the court.

Twice in this letter, Paul reminded his readers that he was a prisoner (Eph. 3:1; 4:1), and at the close he called himself an "ambassador in bonds" (Eph. 6:20). No doubt the Ephesians were asking, "Why is Paul a prisoner in Rome? Why would God permit such a thing?" In this paragraph, Paul explained his situation and, in doing so, also explained one of the greatest truths in this letter, the "mystery" of the church. In the New Testament, a *mystery* is not something eerie or inscrutable, but rather "a truth that was hidden by God in times past and is now revealed to those who are in His family." A *mystery* is a "sacred secret" that is unknown to unbelievers, but understood and treasured by the people of God.

Paul explained the mystery—the Gentile believers are now united to the Jewish believers in one body, the church (Eph. 3:6). He had mentioned this new work of God, so his readers were familiar with the concept (Eph. 1:10; 2:11, 22). But now Paul explained the tremendous impact of this "sacred secret" that had so possessed his own life and ministry. Actually, this explanation is almost a parenthesis in the letter, for Paul began this section with the intention of praying for his readers. Compare Ephesians 3:1 and 14. His use of the words *prisoner* and *Gentiles* led him into this important explanation of the "mystery of the church," and in this explanation, Paul showed us that the "mystery" is important to four different groups of persons.

1. IT WAS IMPORTANT TO PAUL (3:1–5)

The best way to grasp the importance of "the mystery" in Paul's life is to focus on the two descriptions he gave of himself in this section. He began by calling himself "a prisoner" (Eph. 3:1), and then he called himself "a minister" (Eph. 3:7). Paul was a prisoner because he believed in God's new program of uniting believing Jews and Gentiles into one body, the church. The orthodox Jews in Paul's day considered the Gentiles "dogs," but some of the Christian Jews did not have a much better attitude toward the Gentiles.

Paul was a leader in Jewish orthodoxy when Christ saved him (Gal. 1:11–24; Phil. 3:1–11), yet in the providence of God, he began his early ministry in a local church in Antioch that was composed of both Jews and

Gentiles (Acts 11:19–26). When the council was held at Jerusalem to determine the status of believing Gentiles, Paul courageously defended the grace of God and the unity of the church (Acts 15; Gal. 2:1–10).

Paul knew from the very beginning of his Christian life that God had called him to take the gospel to the Gentiles (Acts 9:15; 26:13–18), and he was not disobedient to that call. Wherever Paul ministered, he founded local churches composed of believing Jews and Gentiles, all "one in Christ Jesus" (Gal. 3:28).

Because Paul was the "apostle to the Gentiles" (Rom. 11:13; 15:15–16; Eph. 3:8; 1 Tim. 2:7), he was accused of being prejudiced against the Jews, particularly the Jewish believers in Jerusalem and Judea. The special offering Paul collected for the needy believers in Judea should have shown the goodwill that existed between these churches and the churches Paul founded (Rom. 15:25–33). Paul delivered the offering in person (Acts 21:17–19), and from all evidence, it was graciously received by the Judean Christians. Even though Paul took drastic steps to pacify the Jewish believers, there was a riot in the temple and Paul was arrested (Acts 21:30–33). Paul defended himself by giving his personal testimony, and the crowd listened to him until he got to the word "Gentiles" and then they rioted again (Acts 22:22–23). The rest of the book of Acts explains how Paul got from Jerusalem to Rome, "a prisoner of Jesus Christ for you Gentiles" (Eph. 3:1). Had Paul compromised his message and encouraged the selfish prejudices of the Jews he probably would have been released.

Paul was not only a "prisoner" because of "the mystery," but he was also a "minister." God gave him a "dispensation" (stewardship) that he might go to the Gentiles, not only with the good news of salvation through Christ, but also with the message that Jews and Gentiles are now one in Christ. The word *dispensation* comes from two Greek words: *oikos,* meaning "house" and *nomos,* meaning "law." Our English word *economy* is derived directly from the Greek *oikonomia,* "the law of the house," or "a stewardship, a management." God has different ways of managing His program from age to age, and these different "stewardships" Bible students sometimes call "dispensations" (Eph. 1:9–10). God's principles do not change, but His methods of dealing with humankind do change over the course of history. "Distinguish the ages," wrote Saint Augustine, "and the Scriptures harmonize."

God made Paul a steward of "the mystery" with the responsibility of sharing it with the Gentiles. It was not enough simply to win them to Christ and form them into local assemblies. He was also to teach them their wonderful position in Christ as members of the body, sharing God's grace equally with the Jews. This truth had not been revealed in the Old Testament Scriptures. It was revealed to the New Testament apostles and prophets (see Eph. 4:11) by the Holy Spirit. God revealed it personally to Paul, and it was his responsibility to share it with the Gentile Christians. This was the "dispensation"—or stewardship—that God had given him. And because Paul was a faithful steward, he was now a prisoner in Rome. Like Joseph in the Old Testament, his faithful stewardship resulted in false arrest and imprisonment. But, in the end, it brought great glory to God and salvation to Jews and Gentiles.

2. IT WAS IMPORTANT TO THE GENTILES (3:6–8)

In Ephesians 2:11–22, we discovered that Christ's work on the cross accomplished much more than the salvation of individual sinners. It reconciled Jews and Gentiles to each other and to God. It is this truth that Paul presented here, and you can imagine what exciting news it would be! The truth of "the mystery" reveals to believing Gentiles that they have a wonderful new relationship through Jesus Christ.

To begin with, they are fellow-heirs with the Jews and share in the spiritual riches God gave them because of His covenant with Abraham (Gal. 3:29). In Christ, being a Jew or a Gentile is neither an asset nor a liability, for together we share the riches of Christ. The Gentiles are also fellow-members of the body of Christ, the church. "There is one body" (Eph. 4:4). Our human birth determines our racial distinctions, but our spiritual birth unites us as members of the same body (1 Cor. 12:12–14). Christ is the Head of this body (Eph. 5:22–23), and each individual member shares in the ministry (Eph. 4:10–13). Finally, in their new relationship, the Gentiles are partakers of God's promises. Once they were outside the covenant, with no claims on the promises of God (Eph. 2:12), but now, in Christ, they share the promises of God with the believing Jews. In Romans 11:13–15, Paul explained that believing Gentiles share in the spiritual riches that God gave to Israel. But in Romans 11:1–12, Paul explained that God has not, because of the church, negated His promises to Israel. The church today shares in the spiritual riches of Israel, but one day God will restore His people and fulfill His promises concerning their land and their kingdom.

"The mystery" not only gives believing Gentiles a new relationship, it also reveals that there is a new power available to them (Eph. 3:7). This power is illustrated in the life of Paul. God saved him by grace and gave him a stewardship, a special ministry to the Gentiles. But God also gave Paul the power to accomplish this ministry. The word *working* here is *energeia* from which we get our word *energy*. The word *power* is *dunamis*, which gives us our words *dynamic* and *dynamite*. Paul has already told us about this mighty power in Ephesians 1:19–23, and he will mention it again in Ephesians 3:20 and Ephesians 4:16. The mighty resurrection power of Christ is available to us for daily life and service.

Finally, new riches are available to the Gentiles: "the unsearchable riches of Christ" (Eph. 3:8). Paul called them "exceeding riches" (Eph. 2:7), but here he described them as "unfathomable." The words can also be translated "untraceable," which means that they are so vast you cannot discover their end. (Some students suggest that "untraceable" might also carry the idea that "the mystery" cannot be traced in the Old Testament since it was hidden by God.)

Are these riches available to every believer? Yes! In fact, Paul made it clear that he himself had no special claim on God's wealth, for he considered himself "less than the least of all saints" (Eph. 3:8). The name *Paul* (Paulus) means "little" in Latin, and perhaps Paul bore this name because he realized how insignificant he really was (Acts 13:9). He called himself "the least of the apostles" (1 Cor. 15:9), but at least he was an apostle, which is more than we can claim. Not only does he call himself "less than the least of all saints," but also he calls himself the "chief of sinners" (1 Tim. 1:15). Understanding the deep truths of God's Word does not give a man a big head; it gives him a broken and contrite heart.

3. It Is Important to the Angels (3:9–10)

Perhaps at this point, you are asking yourself the question, "Why did God keep His secret about the church hidden for so many centuries?" Certainly the Old Testament clearly states that God will save the Gentiles through Israel, but nowhere are we told that both Jews and Gentiles will form a new creation, the church, the body of Christ. It was this mystery that the Spirit revealed to Paul and other leaders in the early church, and that was so difficult for the Jews to accept.

Paul told us that "the principalities and powers" are also involved in this great secret. God is "educating" the angels by means of the church! By "the principalities and powers," Paul meant the angelic beings created by God, both good and evil (Eph. 1:21; 6:12; Col. 1:16; 2:15). Angels are created beings and are not omniscient. In fact, Peter indicated that during the Old Testament period, the angels were curious about God's plan of salvation then being worked out on earth (1 Peter 1:10–12). Certainly the angels rejoice at the repentance of a lost sinner (Luke 15:10), and Paul suggested that the angels watch the activities of the local assembly (1 Cor. 11:10). "We are made a spectacle unto the world, and to angels," Paul wrote (1 Cor. 4:9).

What, then, do the angels learn from the church? "The manifold wisdom of God" (Eph. 3:10). Certainly the angels know about the power of God as seen in His creation. But the wisdom of God as seen in His new creation, the church, is something new to them. Unsaved men, including wise philosophers, look at God's plan of salvation and consider it "foolishness" (1 Cor. 1:18–31). But the angels watch the outworking of God's salvation, and they praise His wisdom. Paul called it *manifold wisdom,* and this word carries the idea of "variegated" or "many colored." This suggests the beauty and variety of God's wisdom in His great plan of salvation.

But there is another facet to this truth that must be explored. What are the *evil* angels learning from God's "mystery"? That their leader, Satan, does not have any wisdom! Satan knows the Bible, and he understood from the Old Testament Scriptures *that* the Savior would come, *when* He would come, *how* He would come, and *where* He would come. Satan also understood *why* He would come, as far as redemption is concerned. But nowhere in the Old Testament would Satan find any prophecies concerning the church, "the mystery" of Jews and Gentiles united in one body! Satan could see unbelieving Jews rejecting their Messiah, and he could see Gentiles trusting the Messiah, but he could not see both believing Jews and Gentiles united in one body, seated with Christ in the heavenlies, and completely victorious over Satan! Had Satan known the far-reaching results of the cross, no doubt he would have altered his plans accordingly.

God hid this great plan "from the beginning of the world," but now

He wants "the mystery" to be known by His church. And this is why He made Paul a "steward" of this great truth. Ephesians 3:9 should read, "And to make all men see what is the stewardship of the mystery." Here is an amazing truth: Now *all believers* are to be faithful stewards of this great truth! This "sacred secret" that was so important to Paul, and to the Gentiles, and to angels, is now in *our* hands!

4. IT SHOULD BE IMPORTANT TO CHRISTIANS TODAY (3:11–13)

When God saved Paul, He deposited with him the precious treasures of gospel truth (1 Tim. 1:11). Paul in turn committed these truths to others, exhorting them to commit the truths to faithful men who would guard them and share them (2 Tim. 2:2). "O Timothy, keep that which is committed to thy trust" (1 Tim. 6:20). At the close of his life, Paul would say, to the glory of God, "I have kept the faith" (2 Tim. 4:7). During those apostolic days, the truths of the gospel and "the mystery" were guarded, preached, and handed down to faithful men.

But a study of church history reveals that, one by one, many of the basic truths of the Word of God were lost during the centuries that followed. God had His faithful people—a minority—at all times, but many of the great truths of the Word were buried under man-made theology, tradition, and ritual. Then, God's Spirit began to open the eyes of seeking souls, and these great truths were unveiled again. Martin Luther championed justification by faith. Other spiritual leaders rediscovered the person and work of the Holy Spirit, the glorious truth of the return of Jesus Christ, and the joy of the victorious Christian life. In recent years, the truth of "the mystery" has again excited the hearts of God's people. We rejoice that we are "all one in Christ Jesus."

Most of us identify Napoleon Bonaparte as the would-be conqueror of Europe. But not many would name him as a patron of arts and sciences. Yet he was. In July 1798, Napoleon began to occupy Egypt, but by September 1801, he was forced to get out. Those three years meant failure as far as his military and political plans were concerned, but they meant success in one area that greatly interested him—archeology. For in August 1799, a Frenchman named Boussand discovered the Rosetta Stone about thirty miles from Alexandria. This discovery gave to archeologists the key to understanding Egyptian hieroglyphics. It opened the door to modern Egyptian studies.

The "mystery" is God's "Rosetta Stone." It is the key to what He promised in the Old Testament, what Christ did in the Gospels, what the early church did in the book of Acts, what Paul and the other writers teach in the Epistles, and what God will do as recorded in the book of Revelation. God's program today is not "the headship of Israel" (Deut. 28:1–13), but the headship of Christ over His church. We today are under a different "stewardship" from that of Moses and the Prophets, and we must be careful not to confuse what God has clarified.

The reason many churches are weak and ineffective is because they do not understand what they have in Christ. And the cause of this is often spiritual leaders who are not good "stewards of the mystery." Because they do not "rightly divide the word of truth" (2 Tim. 2:15), they confuse their people concerning their spiritual position in Christ, and they rob their people of the spiritual wealth in Christ.

This great truth concerning the church is not a divine afterthought. It is a part of God's eternal purpose in Christ (Eph. 3:11). To ignore this truth is to sin against the Father who planned it, the Son whose death made it possible, and the Spirit who today seeks to work in our lives to accomplish what God has planned. When you understand this truth, it gives you great confidence and faith (Eph. 3:12). When you know what God is doing in the world, and you work with Him, you can be sure that He will work *in* you and *for* you. All of His divine resources are available to those who sincerely want to do His will and help Him accomplish His purposes on earth.

The early church thought that the gospel belonged to the Jews because it had come *through* them and *to* them first. Until Peter, by divine direction, went to the Gentiles in Acts 10, the Jewish believers thought that a Gentile had to become a Jew before he could become a Christian! God's Spirit gradually revealed to the churches that God was doing a new thing: He was calling out a people for His name from both the Jews and Gentiles (Acts 15:14). There are no national, racial, political, physical, or social distinctions in the church! "There is neither Jew nor Greek, there is neither bond nor free, there is neither male nor female: For ye are all one in Christ Jesus" (Gal. 3:28).

But an understanding of God's program in this present age not only gives the believer confidence toward God. It also gives him courage in the difficult circumstances of life. Paul's sufferings for the Gentiles would mean glory for the Gentiles. In the Old Testament age, when God's people obeyed, God blessed them materially, nationally, and physically (Deut. 28), and if they disobeyed, He withdrew these blessings. This is not the way He deals with the church today. Our blessings are spiritual, not material (Eph. 1:3); they have *all* been given to us completely in Christ. We appropriate them by faith, but if we disobey God, He does not revoke them. We simply lose the enjoyment and the enrichment of them. Paul was certainly a dedicated, Spirit-filled man, yet he was suffering as a prisoner. Paul made it clear that physical, material blessings are not always the experience of the dedicated Christian (2 Cor. 4:7–12; 11:23—12:10).

I was driving to a preaching engagement, trying to follow a map I had found in the glove compartment of my car. (I am a very poor navigator, so my wife is usually the navigator in our family.) For some reason, I could not locate the interstate highway I needed, so I stopped to get directions at a filling station.

"You've got an ancient map there, Mister!" the attendant told me. "Here's the latest map. Follow it and you'll get where you are going." He was right. I followed the new map and arrived in plenty of time to preach.

People who do not understand God's "mystery" in His church are trying to make spiritual progress with the wrong map. Or, to change the figure, they are trying to build with the wrong blueprints. God's churches on this earth—the local assemblies—are not supposed to be either Gentile culture cliques or Jewish culture cliques. For a German church to refuse fellowship to a Swede is just as unscriptural as for a Jewish congregation to refuse a Gentile. God's church is not to be shackled by culture, class, or any other physical distinction. It is a spiritual entity that must submit to the headship of Jesus Christ in the power of the Spirit.

Yes, God had a "secret"—but God does not want it to be a secret anymore! If you understand your wonderful position in Christ, then live up to it—and share the blessing with others. This "secret" was important to Paul, to the Gentiles, and to the angels—and it ought to be important to you and me today.

QUESTIONS FOR PERSONAL REFLECTION
OR GROUP DISCUSSION

1. Read Ephesians 3:1–13. Paul speaks of a mystery: that Gentiles are now welcome in the family of God. Why was this such a big deal?

2. Is the reconciliation between Jews and Gentiles old news, or does it matter today? Explain.

3. What are some of the riches of Judaism that Gentiles have access to in Christ?

4. What do the angels learn from this revealed mystery (3:9–10)? How does it affect you to think about that?

5. How is this passage related to 2:11–22?

6. One of the themes running through Ephesians is God's power (3:7), the power that raised Jesus from the dead (1:19–21) and is still at work in the world. What did God's power do for Paul? What has it done for you?

7. God's welcome to the Gentiles is supposed to give us boldness and confidence to approach God (3:12). How confident are you about approaching God? Explain.

8. Why do you think some believers and churches lack the confidence God wants them to have?

9. How does knowing this mystery strengthen you today?

Chapter Seven

GET YOUR HANDS ON YOUR WEALTH

(Ephesians 3:14–21)

This passage is the second of two prayers recorded in Ephesians, the first one being Ephesians 1:15–23. In the first prayer, the emphasis is on *enlightenment,* but in this prayer, the emphasis is on *enablement.* It is not so much a matter of *knowing* as *being*—laying our hands on what God has for us and by faith making it a vital part of our lives. Paul was saying, "I want you to get your hands on your wealth, realize how vast it is, and start to use it."

It is worth noting that both of these prayers, as well as the other prison prayers (Phil. 1:9–11; Col. 1:9–12), deal with the spiritual condition of the inner man, and not the material needs of the body. Certainly it is not wrong to pray for physical and material needs, but the emphasis in these petitions is on the spiritual. Paul knew that if the inner man is what he ought to be, the outer man will be taken care of in due time. Too many of our prayers focus only on physical and material needs and fail to lay hold of the deeper inner needs of the heart. It would do us good to use these prison prayers as our own, and ask God to help us in our inner person. That is where the greatest needs are.

THE INVOCATION (3:14–15)

The first thing that strikes us is Paul's posture: "I bow my knees." (This must have been quite an experience for the Roman soldier chained to Paul!) The Bible nowhere commands any special posture for prayer. Abraham stood before the Lord when he prayed for Sodom (Gen. 18:22), and Solomon stood when he prayed to dedicate the temple (1 Kings 8:22). David "sat before the Lord" (1 Chron. 17:16) when he prayed about the future of his kingdom. And Jesus "fell on his face" when He prayed in Gethsemane (Matt. 26:39).

You have noticed, no doubt, the emphasis on spiritual posture in Ephesians. As lost sinners, we were buried in the graveyard (Eph. 2:1). But when we trusted Christ, He raised us from the dead and seated us with Christ in the heavenlies (Eph. 2:4–6). Because we are *seated* with Christ, we can *walk* so as to please Him (Eph. 4:1, 17; 5:2, 8, 15) and we can *stand* against the Devil (Eph. 6:10–13). But the posture that links "sitting" with "walking" and "standing" is "bowing the knee." It is through prayer that we lay hold of God's riches that enable us to behave like Christians and battle like Christians. Whether we actually bow our knees is not the important thing; that we bow our hearts and wills to the Lord and ask Him for what we need is the vital matter.

Paul's prayer was addressed to "the Father of our Lord Jesus Christ." In the Bible, prayer is addressed to the Father, through the Son, and in the Spirit. This is the usual pattern, though you do find petitions addressed to the Son, and possibly to the Spirit (1 Thess. 3:12–13). In Ephesians 1:3, Paul called the Father "the God and Father of our Lord Jesus Christ." He was the "God … of our Lord Jesus Christ" when Jesus was here on earth, for as man, Jesus lived in total dependence on God. This title reminds us of Christ's humanity. But God is the "Father of our Lord Jesus Christ" because Jesus Christ is eternal God; so this title reminds us of His deity.

There is a sense, however, in which all men in general, and Christians in particular, share in the fatherhood of God. Paul stated that "the whole family in heaven and earth is named" after the divine Father. That word *family* can be translated "fatherhood." Every fatherhood in heaven and on earth gets its origin and name from the Father. He is the great Original; every other fatherhood is but a copy. Adam is called "the son of God" (Luke 3:38), referring to his creation. Believers are the "sons of God" by rebirth (John 1:11–13; 1 John 3:1–2). All men are not children of God by nature. Instead, they are children of disobedience and children of wrath (Eph. 2:2–3). As Creator, God is the Father of each person, but as Savior, He is only the Father of those who believe. There is no such thing in Scripture as the universal fatherhood of God that saves all men. "Ye must be born again" (John 3:7).

THE PETITION (3:16–19)

There are four requests in Paul's prayer, but they must not be looked on as isolated, individual petitions. These four requests are more like four parts to a telescope. One request leads into the next one, and so on. He prays that the inner man might have spiritual strength, which will, in turn, lead to a deeper experience with Christ. This deeper experience will enable them to "apprehend" (get hold of) God's great love, which will result in their being "filled unto all the fullness of God." So, then, Paul was praying for strength, depth, apprehension, and fullness.

Strength (v. 16). The presence of the Holy Spirit in the life is evidence of salvation (Rom. 8:9); but the power of the Spirit is enablement for Christian living, and it is this power that Paul desired for his readers. "Ye shall receive power, when the Holy Spirit is come upon you" (Acts 1:8, literal translation). Jesus performed His ministry on earth in the power of the Spirit (Luke 4:1, 14; Acts 10:38), and this is the only resource we have for Christian living today. As you read the book of Acts, you see the importance of the Holy Spirit in the life of the church, for there are some fifty-nine references to the Spirit in the book, or one fourth of the total references found in the New Testament. Someone has said, "If God took the Holy Spirit out of this world, most of what we Christians are doing would go right on—and nobody would know the difference!" Sad, but true.

The power of the Spirit is given to us "according to the riches of his glory" (Eph. 3:16). Christ returned to glory and sent the Spirit from heaven to indwell and empower His people. It is not necessary for us to "work something up." The power has to be sent down. How marvelous that God does not give the Spirit's power to us "out of his riches," but "according to"—which is a far greater thing. If I am a billionaire and I give you ten dollars, I have given you *out of* my riches; but if I give you a million dollars, I have given to you *according to* my riches. The first is a *portion;* the second is a *proportion.*

This power is available for "the inner man." This means the spiritual part of man where God dwells and works. The inner man of the lost sinner is dead (Eph. 2:1), but it becomes alive when Christ is invited in. The inner man can see (Ps. 119:18), hear (Matt. 13:9), taste (Ps. 34:8), and feel (Acts 17:27), and he must be "exercised" (1 Tim. 4:7–8). He also must be cleansed (Ps. 51:7) and fed (Matt. 4:4). The outer man is perishing, but the inner man can be renewed spiritually in spite of outward physical decay (2 Cor. 4:16–18). It is this inner power that makes him succeed.

What does it mean to have the Holy Spirit empower the inner man? It means that our spiritual faculties are controlled by God, and we are exercising them and growing in the Word (Heb. 5:12–14). It is only when we yield to the Spirit and let Him control the inner man that we succeed in living to the glory of God. This means feeding the inner man the Word of God, praying and worshipping, keeping clean, and exercising the senses by loving obedience.

Depth (v. 17). Paul used three pictures here to convey this idea of spiritual depth, and the three pictures are hidden in the three verbs: "dwell," "rooted," and "grounded." The verb *dwell* literally means (and here I follow Dr. Kenneth Wuest) "to settle down and feel at home." Certainly Christ was already resident in the hearts of the Ephesians, or else Paul would not have addressed them as "saints" in Ephesians 1:1. What Paul was praying for was a deeper experience between Christ and His people. He yearned for Christ to settle down and feel at home in their hearts—not a surface relationship, but an ever-deepening fellowship.

Abraham's life is an illustration of this truth. God was going to bless Abraham with a son, so the Lord Himself came down and visited Abraham's tent, and He brought two angels with Him. They came to the tent, they talked with Abraham, and they even ate a meal with him. They felt very much at home, because Abraham was a man of faith and obedience. But the three guests had another task. They had to investigate the sins of Sodom because God planned to destroy the cities of Sodom and Gomorrah. Lot, a believer, was living in Sodom, and God wanted to warn him to get out before the judgment could fall. But the Lord Himself did not go to Sodom. He sent the two angels (Gen. 18—19). The Lord did not feel at home in Lot's house the way He felt at home in Abraham's tent.

The verb *rooted* moves us into the plant world. The tree must get its roots deep into the soil if it is to have both nourishment and stability, and the Christian must have his spiritual roots deep into the love of God. Psalm 1:1–3 is a perfect description of this word, and Jeremiah 17:5–8 is a good commentary on it. One of the most important questions a Christian can ask himself is, "From what do I draw my nourishment and my stability?" If there is to be power in the Christian life, then there must be depth. The roots must go deeper and deeper into the love of Christ.

Grounded is an architectural term; it refers to the foundations on which we build. In the first two churches I pastored, we were privileged to construct new buildings, and in both projects it seemed we would never get out of the ground. In my second building program, we had to spend several thousand dollars taking soil tests because we were building over an old lake bed. For weeks, the men were laying out and pouring the footings. One day I complained to the architect, and he replied, "Pastor, the most important part of this building is the foundation. If you don't go deep, you can't go high." That sentence has been a sermon to me ever since.

The trials of life test the depth of our experience. If two roommates in college have a falling out, they may seek new roommates, for after all, living with a roommate is a passing experience. But if a husband and wife, who love each other, have a disagreement, the trial only deepens their love as they seek to solve the problems. The storm that blows reveals the strength of the roots. Jesus told the story about the two builders, one of whom did not go deep enough for his foundation (Matt. 7:24–29). Paul prayed that the believers might have a deeper experience with Christ, because only a deep experience could sustain them during the severe trials of life.

Apprehension (vv. 18–19a). The English words *comprehend* and *apprehend* both stem from the Latin word *prehendere* which means "to grasp." We say that a monkey has a "prehensile tail." That is, its tail is able to grasp a tree limb and hold on. Our word *comprehend* carries the idea of mentally grasping something; while *apprehend* suggests laying hold of it for yourself. In other words, it is possible to understand something but not really make it your own. Paul's concern was that we lay hold of the vast expanses of the love of God. He wanted us to live in four dimensions. When God gave the land to Abraham, He told him to "walk through the land in the length of it and in the breadth of it" (Gen. 13:17). Abraham had to step out by faith and claim his inheritance. But we today have an inheritance in four dimensions: breadth, length, depth, and height. God's fourth dimension is love!

But there is a paradox here. Paul wanted us to know personally the love of Christ "which passeth knowledge." There are dimensions, but they cannot be measured. "The love of Christ which passeth knowledge" parallels "the unsearchable riches of Christ" (Eph. 3:8). We are so rich in Christ that our riches cannot be calculated even with the most sophisticated computer.

Perhaps you saw the cartoon that depicted a man chatting with a boat salesman. In the beautiful showroom were yachts and cabin cruisers that glittered with elegance. In the caption, the salesman is saying to the customer, "Sir, if you have to ask how much they are, they are too expensive for you!"

No Christian ever has to worry about having inadequate spiritual resources to meet the demands of life. If he prays for spiritual strength and spiritual depth, he will be able to apprehend—get his hands on—all the resources of God's love and grace. "I can do all things through Christ which strengtheneth me" (Phil. 4:13). And what is the result of all of this?

Fullness (v. 19b). It is said that nature abhors a vacuum. This explains why air or water will automatically flow into an empty place. The *divine* nature abhors a vacuum. God wants us to experience His fullness. "Filled *unto* all the fullness of God" is the more accurate translation. The *means* of our fullness is the Holy Spirit (Eph. 5:18), and the *measure* of our fullness is God Himself (Eph. 4:11–16). It is tragic when Christians use the wrong measurements in examining their own spiritual lives. We like to measure ourselves by the weakest Christians that we know, and then boast, "Well, I'm better than they are." Paul tells us that the measure is Christ, and that we cannot boast about anything (nor should we). When we have reached *His* fullness, then we have reached the limit.

In one sense, the Christian is already "made full in Christ" (Col. 2:9–10, where "complete" means "filled full"). Positionally, we are complete in Him, but practically, we enjoy only the grace that we apprehend by faith. The resources are there. All we need do is accept them and enjoy them. Paul will have more to say about this fullness (Eph. 5:18–21), so we will reserve further comment until we reach that section.

THE BENEDICTION (3:20–21)

After contemplating such a marvelous spiritual experience, it is no wonder Paul burst forth in a doxology, a fitting benediction to such a prayer. Note again the trinitarian emphasis in this benediction: Paul prayed to God the Father, concerning the indwelling power of God the Spirit, made available through God the Son.

Perhaps the best way for us to grasp some of the greatness of this doxology is to look at it in outlined form:

> Now unto Him that is
> able to do *all*
> *above* all
> *abundantly* above all
> *exceeding* abundantly above all

Paul seemed to want to use every word possible to convey to us the vastness of God's power as found in Jesus Christ. He ended each of the two previous chapters with praise to God for His great victory in Christ. He told us that Christ's power is so great He arose from the dead and ascended *far above all* (Eph. 1:19–23). He taught us that His power is so great He has reconciled Jews and Gentiles to each other, and to God, and that He is now building a temple to the eternal glory of God (Eph. 2:19–22). But in the paragraph before us, Paul shared the exciting truth that this *far above all* power is available to us! It is even "above all that we ask or think." In other words, the power of Christ, like the love of Christ, is beyond human understanding or measurement. And this is just the kind of power you and I need if we are to walk and war in victory.

The word *power* is again *dunamis,* which we met back in Ephesians 3:7, and *working* is *energeia* (energy) found in Ephesians 1:11, 19; 2:2; 3:7; and 4:16. Some power is dormant; it is available, but not being used, such as the power stored in a battery. But God's energy is effectual power—power at work in our lives. This power works *in* us, in the inner man (Eph. 3:16). Philippians 2:12–13 are parallel verses, so be sure to read them. It is the Holy Spirit who releases the resurrection power of Christ in our lives.

One winter day, I had an important engagement in Chicago, and the evening before, the area was hit by a severe snowstorm. I did not have a garage, so my car was not only covered with snow, but heavy cakes of ice had formed under the fenders and bumpers. These ice cakes I simply kicked off, after I had swept off the car. I drove to the gas station to fill the tank. When I pushed the button on the dashboard to open the gas cap, it didn't work. No matter how hard or often I pushed, the cap stayed shut. The station attendant looked under the fender and discovered the problem. In kicking off the ice, I had broken the wire that connected the gas cap with the battery.

Apparently this is what has happened to many Christians. They have been cut off from their source of power. Unbelief, unconfessed sin, careless living, worldliness in action or attitude—all of these can rob us of power. And a Christian robbed of power cannot be used of God. "Without me ye can do nothing" (John 15:5).

Why does God share His power with us? So that we can build great churches for our own glory? So that we can boast of our own achievements? No! "To him be glory in the church!" The Spirit of God was given to glorify the Son of God (John 16:14). The church on earth is here to glorify the Son of God. If our motive is to glorify God by building His church, then God will share His power with us. The power of the Spirit is not a luxury; it is a necessity.

But the amazing thing is that what we do in His power today will glorify Christ "throughout all ages, world without end" (Eph. 3:21). The church's greatest ministry is yet to come. What we do here and now is preparing us for the eternal ages, when we shall glorify Christ forever.

He is able to do all—*above* all—*abundantly* above all—*exceeding* abundantly above all!

Get your hands on your spiritual wealth by opening your heart to the Holy Spirit, and praying with Paul for strength for the inner man ... for a new depth of love ... for spiritual apprehension ... and for spiritual fullness.

"Ye have not, because ye ask not" (James 4:2).

QUESTIONS FOR PERSONAL REFLECTION
OR GROUP DISCUSSION

1. Think about your prayers the past several days. How do you think God would evaluate them? Why?

2. Read Paul's second recorded prayer for the Ephesians in 3:14–19. Why did he kneel to God in prayer?

3. Paul prayed that they would be strengthened with power through the Holy Spirit. If you've ever prayed for strength, what did you want the strength for?

4. What did Paul want his readers to have the strength to do? Why did that require strength?

5. How does the Holy Spirit strengthen our inner beings?

6. Why is it necessary for a Christian to be rooted and grounded in love? Whose love for whom?

7. How strongly aware are you of Christ's incomprehensible love for you? What is the evidence in your outlook on life and your habits?

8. How does a person grow in awareness of Christ's love for him or her?

9. What is God's fullness? How can we experience it in practical ways?

10. How are the four requests in Paul's prayer related?

11. What impressed you most about Paul's prayer? Why?

Chapter Eight

LET'S WALK TOGETHER

(Ephesians 4:1–16)

A ll of Paul's letters contain a beautiful balance between doctrine and duty, and Ephesians is the perfect example. The first three chapters deal with doctrine, our riches in Christ, while the last three chapters explain duty, our responsibilities in Christ. The key word in this last half of the book is *walk* (Eph. 4:1, 17; 5:2, 8, 15), while the key idea in the first half is wealth. In these last three chapters, Paul admonished us to walk in *unity* (Eph. 4:1–16), *purity* (Eph. 4:17—5:17), *harmony* (Eph. 5:18—6:9), and *victory* (Eph. 6:10–24).

These four "walks" perfectly parallel the basic doctrines Paul has taught us in the first three chapters.

Before we look at this section in detail, we must note two important words in Ephesians 4:1: *therefore* and *beseech*. The word *therefore* indicates that Paul was basing his exhortations to duty on the doctrines taught in the first three chapters. (Rom. 12:1–2 are parallel verses.) The Christian life is not based on ignorance but knowledge, and the better we understand Bible doctrine, the easier it is to obey Bible duties. When people say, "Don't talk to me about doctrine—just let me live my Christian life!" they are revealing their ignorance of the way the Holy Spirit works in the life of the believer. "It makes no difference what you believe, just as long as you live right" is a similar confession of ignorance. It *does* make a difference what you believe, because what you believe determines how you behave!

Our Wealth	*Our Walk*
Called by grace to belong to His body (ch. 1)	Walk worthy of your calling— the unity of the body (4:1–16)
Raised from the dead (2:1–10)	Put off the graveclothes (4:17–5:17); walk in purity
Reconciled (2:11–22)	Walk in harmony (5:18—6:9)
Christ's victory over Satan is the mystery (ch. 3)	Walk in victory (6:10–24)

The word *beseech* indicates that God, in love, urges us to live for His glory. He does not say, as He did to the Old Testament Jews, "If you obey Me, I will bless you." Rather, He says, "I have already blessed you—now, in response to My love and grace, obey Me." He has given us such a marvelous calling in Christ; now it is our responsibility to live up to that calling.

The main idea in these first sixteen verses is the unity of believers in Christ. This is simply the practical application of the doctrine taught in the first half of the letter: God is building a body, a temple. He has reconciled Jews and Gentiles to Himself in Christ. The oneness of believers in Christ is already a spiritual reality. Our responsibility is to guard, protect, and preserve that unity. To do this, we must understand four important facts.

1. THE GRACE OF UNITY (4:1–3)

Unity is not uniformity. Unity comes from within and is a spiritual grace, while uniformity is the result of pressure from without. Paul used the human body as a picture of Christian unity (1 Cor. 12), and he adapted the same illustration here in this section (Eph. 4:13–16). Each part of the body is different from the other parts, yet all make up one body and work together.

If we are going to preserve the "unity of the Spirit," we must possess the necessary Christian graces, and there are six of them listed here. The first is *lowliness,* or *humility.* Someone has said, "Humility is that grace that, when you know you have it, you have lost it." Humility means putting Christ first, others second, and self last. It means knowing ourselves, accepting ourselves, and being ourselves to the glory of God. God does not condemn you when you accept yourself and your gifts (Rom. 12:3). He just does not want us to think more *highly* of ourselves than we ought to—or *less highly* than we ought to.

Meekness is not weakness. It is power under control. Moses was a meek man (Num. 12:3), yet see the tremendous power he exercised. Jesus Christ was "meek and lowly in heart" (Matt. 11:29), yet He drove the money-changers from the temple. In the Greek language, this word was used for a soothing medicine, a colt that had been broken, and a soft wind. In each case you have power, but that power is under control.

Allied with meekness is *longsuffering,* which literally means "long-tempered," the ability to endure discomfort without fighting back. This leads to the mentioning of *forbearance,* a grace that cannot be experienced apart from love. "Charity suffereth long, and is kind" (1 Cor. 13:4). Actually, Paul was describing some of the "fruit of the Spirit" (Gal. 5:22–23); for the "unity of the Spirit" (Eph. 4:3) is the result of the believer "walking in the Spirit" (Gal. 5:16).

The next grace that contributes to the unity of the Spirit is *endeavor.* Literally it reads "being eager to maintain, or guard, the unity of the Spirit." "It's great that you love each other," I once heard a seasoned saint say to a newly wedded couple, "but if you're going to be happy in marriage, you gotta work at it!" The verb used here is a present participle, which means we must constantly be endeavoring to maintain this unity. In fact, when we think the situation is the best, Satan will move in to wreck it. The spiritual unity of a home, a Sunday school class, or a church is the responsibility of each person involved, and the job never ends.

The final grace is *peace*—"the bond of peace." Read James 3:13—4:10 for the most vivid treatment of war and peace in the New Testament. Note that the reason for war on the outside is war on the inside. If a believer cannot get along with God, he cannot get along with other believers. When "the peace of God" rules in our hearts, then we build unity (Col. 3:15).

2. THE GROUNDS OF UNITY (4:4–6)

Many people today attempt to unite Christians in a way that is not biblical. For example, they will say, "We are not interested in doctrines, but in love. Now, let's forget our doctrines and just love one another!" But Paul did not discuss spiritual unity in the first three chapters; he waited until he had laid the doctrinal foundation. While not all Christians agree on some minor matters of Christian doctrine, they all do agree on the foundation truths of the faith. Unity built on anything other than Bible truth is standing on a very shaky foundation. Paul names here the seven basic spiritual realities that unite all true Christians.

One body. This is, of course, the body of Christ in which each believer is a member, placed there at conversion by the Spirit of God (1 Cor. 12:12–31). The one body is the model for the many local bodies that God has established across the world. The fact that a person is a member of the one body does not excuse him from belonging to a local body, for it is there that he exercises his spiritual gifts and helps others to grow.

One Spirit. The same Holy Spirit indwells each believer, so that we belong to each other in the Lord. There are perhaps a dozen references to the Holy Spirit in Ephesians, because He is important to us in the living of the Christian life.

One hope of your calling. This refers to the return of the Lord to take His church to heaven. The Holy Spirit within is the assurance of this great promise (Eph. 1:13–14). Paul was suggesting here that the believer who realizes the existence of the one body, who walks in the Spirit, and who looks for the Lord's return, is going to be a peacemaker and not a troublemaker.

One Lord. This is our Lord Jesus Christ, who died for us, lives for us, and one day will come for us. It is difficult to believe that two believers can claim to obey the same Lord, and yet not be able to walk together in unity. Someone asked Ghandi, the spiritual leader of India, "What is the greatest hindrance to Christianity in India?" He replied, "Christians." Acknowledging the lordship of Christ is a giant step toward spiritual unity among His people.

One faith. There is one settled body of truth deposited by Christ in His church, and this is "the faith." Jude called it "the faith which was once delivered unto the saints" (Jude 3). The early Christians recognized a body of basic doctrine that they taught, guarded, and committed to others (2 Tim. 2:2). Christians may differ in some matters of interpretation and church practice, but all true Christians agree on "the faith"—and to depart from "the faith" is to bring about disunity within the body of Christ.

One baptism. Since Paul was here discussing the one body, this "one baptism" is probably the baptism of the Spirit, that act of the Spirit when He places the believing sinner into the body of Christ at conversion (1 Cor. 12:13). This is not an experience after conversion, nor is it an experience the believer should pray for or seek after. We are commanded to be filled with the Spirit (Eph. 5:18), but we are never commanded to be baptized with the Spirit, for we have already been baptized by the Spirit at conversion. As far as the one body is concerned, there is one baptism—the baptism of the Spirit. But as far as local bodies of believers are concerned, there are two baptisms: the baptism of the Spirit and water baptism.

One God and Father. Paul liked to emphasize God as Father (Eph. 1:3, 17; 2:18; 3:14; 5:20). The marvelous oneness of believers in the family of God is evident here, for God is over all, and working through all, and in all. We are children in the same family, loving and serving the same Father, so we ought to be able to walk together in unity. Just as in an earthly family the various members have to give and take in order to keep a loving unity in the home, so God's heavenly family must do the same. The "Lord's Prayer" opens with "Our Father"—not "My Father."

Paul was quite concerned that Christians not break the unity of the Spirit by agreeing with false doctrine (Rom. 16:17–20), and the apostle John echoed this warning (2 John 6–11). The local church cannot believe in peace at any price, for God's wisdom is "first pure, then peaceable" (James 3:17). Purity of doctrine of itself does not produce spiritual unity, for there are churches that are sound in faith, but unsound when it comes to love. This is why Paul joined the two: "speaking the truth in love" (Eph. 4:15).

3. The Gifts for Unity (4:7–11)

Paul moved now from what all Christians have in common to how Christians differ from each other. He was discussing variety and individuality within the unity of the Spirit. God has given each believer at least one spiritual gift (1 Cor. 12:1–12), and this gift is to be used for the unifying and edifying (building up) of the body of Christ. We must make a distinction between "spiritual gifts" and natural abilities. When you were born into this world God gave you certain natural abilities, perhaps in mechanics, art, athletics, or music. In this regard, all men are not created equal, because some are smarter, or stronger, or more talented than others. But in the spiritual realm, each believer has at least one spiritual gift no matter what natural abilities he may or may not possess. A spiritual gift is a God-given ability to serve God and other Christians in such a way that Christ is glorified and believers are edified.

How does the believer discover and develop his gifts? By fellowshipping with other Christians in the local assembly. Gifts are not toys to play with. They are tools to build with. And if they are not used in love, they become weapons to fight with, which is what happened in the Corinthian church (1 Cor. 12—14). Christians are not to live in isolation, for after all, they are members of the same body.

Paul taught that Christ is the Giver of these gifts, through the Holy Spirit (Eph. 4:8–10). He ascended to heaven as Victor forevermore. The picture here is of a military conqueror leading his captives and sharing the spoil with his followers. Only in this case, the "captives" are not His enemies, but His own. Sinners who once were held captives by sin and Satan have now been taken captive by Christ. Even death itself is a defeated foe! When He came to earth, Christ experienced the depths of humiliation (Phil. 2:5–11), but when He ascended to heaven, He experienced the very highest exaltation possible. Paul quoted Psalm 68:18, applying to Jesus Christ a victory song written by David (Eph. 4:8).

There are three lists of spiritual gifts given in the New Testament: 1 Corinthians 12:4–11, 27–31; Romans 12:3–8; and Ephesians 4:11. Since these lists are not identical, it may be that Paul has not named all the gifts that are available. Paul wrote that some gifts are more important than others, but that all believers are needed if the body is to function normally (1 Cor. 14:5, 39). Paul named, not so much "gifts" as the gifted men God has placed in the church, and there are four of them.

Apostles (v. 11a). The word means "one who is sent with a commission." Jesus had many disciples, but He selected twelve apostles (Matt. 10:1–4).

A *disciple* is a "follower" or a "learner," but an *apostle* is a "divinely appointed representative." The apostles were to give witness of the resurrection (Acts 1:15–22), and therefore had to have seen the risen Christ personally (1 Cor. 9:1–2). There are no apostles today in the strictest New Testament sense. These men helped to lay the foundation of the church—"the foundation of the apostles and prophets" (Eph. 2:20), and once the foundation was laid, they were no longer needed. God authenticated their ministry with special miracles (Heb. 2:1–4), so we should not demand these same miracles today. Of course, in a broad sense, all Christians have an apostolic ministry. "As my Father hath sent me, even so send I you" (John 20:21). But we must not claim to be apostles.

Prophets (v. 11b). We commonly associate a prophet with predictions of future events, but this is not his primary function. A New Testament prophet is one who proclaims the Word of God (Acts 11:28; Eph. 3:5). Believers in the New Testament churches did not possess Bibles, nor was the New Testament written and completed. How, then, would these local assemblies discover God's will? His Spirit would share God's truth with those possessing the gift of prophecy. Paul suggested that the gift of prophecy had to do with understanding "all mysteries, and all knowledge" (1 Cor. 13:2), meaning, of course, spiritual truths. The purpose of prophecy is "edification, encouragement, and consolation" (1 Cor. 14:3, literal translation). Christians today do not get their spiritual knowledge *immediately* from the Holy Spirit, but *mediately* through the Spirit teaching the Word. With the apostles, the prophets had a foundational ministry in the early church, and they are not needed today (Eph. 2:20).

Evangelists (v. 11c). "Bearers of the good news." These men traveled from place to place to preach the gospel and win the lost (Acts 8:26–40; 21:28). All ministers should "do the work of an evangelist," but this does not mean that all ministers are evangelists (2 Tim. 4:5). The apostles and prophets laid the foundation of the church, and the evangelists built on it by winning the lost to Christ. Of course, in the early church, every believer was a witness (Acts 2:41–47; 11:19–21), and so should we be witnesses today. But there are people also today who have the gift of evangelism. The fact that a believer may not possess this gift does not excuse him from being burdened for lost souls or witnessing to them.

Pastors and teachers (v. 11d). The fact that the word *some* is not repeated indicates that we have here one office with two ministries. *Pastor* means "shepherd," indicating that the local church is a flock of sheep (Acts 20:28), and it is his responsibility to feed and lead the flock (1 Peter 5:1–4, where "elder" is another name for "pastor"). He does this by means of the Word of God, the food that nourishes the sheep. The Word is the staff that guides and disciplines the sheep. The Word of God is the local church's protection and provision, and no amount of entertainment, good fellowship, or other religious substitutes can take its place.

4. THE GROWTH OF UNITY (4:12–16)

Paul was looking at the church on two levels in this section. He saw the body of Christ, made up of all true believers, growing gradually until it reaches spiritual maturity, "the measure of the stature of the fullness of Christ." But he also saw the local body of believers ministering to each other, growing together, and thereby experiencing spiritual unity.

A freelance missionary visited a pastor friend of mine asking for financial support. "What group are you associated with?" my friend asked.

The man replied, "I belong to the invisible church."

My friend then asked, "Well, what church are you a member of?"

Again he got the answer, "I belong to the invisible church!"

Getting a bit suspicious, my friend asked, "When does this invisible church meet? Who pastors it?"

The missionary then became incensed and said, "Well, your church here isn't the true church. I belong to the invisible church!"

My friend replied, "Well, here's some invisible money to help you minister to the invisible church!"

Now, my pastor friend was not denying the existence of the one body. Rather, he was affirming the fact that the *invisible church* (not a biblical term, but I will use it) ministers *through* the visible church.

The gifted leaders are supposed to "equip the saints unto the work of the ministry, unto the building up of the body of Christ" (literal translation). The saints do not call a pastor and pay him to do the work. They call him and follow his leadership as he, through the Word, equips them to do the job (2 Tim. 3:13–17). The members of the church grow by feeding on the Word and ministering to each other. The first evidence of spiritual growth is *Christlikeness.*

The second evidence is *stability.* The maturing Christian is not tossed about by every religious novelty that comes along. There are religious quacks waiting to kidnap God's children and get them into their false cults, but the maturing believer recognizes false doctrine and stays clear of it. The cultists do not try to win lost souls to Christ. They do not establish rescue missions in the slum areas of our cities, because they have no good news for the man on skid row. Instead, these false teachers try to capture immature Christians, and for this reason, most of the membership of the false cults comes from local churches, particularly churches that do not feed their people the Word of God.

The third evidence of maturity is *truth joined with love:* "Speaking the truth in love" (Eph. 4:15). It has well been said that truth without love is brutality, but love without truth is hypocrisy. Little children do not know how to blend truth and love. They think that if you love someone, you must shield him from the truth if knowing the truth will hurt him. It is a mark of maturity when we are able to share the truth with our fellow Christians, and do it in love. "Faithful are the wounds of a friend; but the kisses of an enemy are deceitful" (Prov. 27:6).

One more evidence of maturity is *cooperation* (Eph. 4:16). We realize that, as members of the one body and a local body, we belong to each other, we affect each other, and we need each other. Each believer, no matter how insignificant he may appear, has a ministry to other believers. The body grows as the individual members grow, and they grow as they feed on the Word and minister to each other. Note once again the emphasis on love: "forbearing one another in love" (Eph. 4:2); "speaking the truth in love" (Eph. 4:15); "the edifying of itself in love" (4:16). Love is the circulatory system of the body. It has been discovered that isolated, unloved babies do not grow properly and are especially susceptible to disease, while babies who are loved and handled grow normally and are stronger. So it is with the children of God. An isolated Christian cannot minister to others, nor can others minister to him, and it is impossible for the gifts to be ministered either way.

So, then, spiritual unity is not something we manufacture. It is something we already have in Christ, and we must protect and maintain it. Truth unites, but lies divide. Love unites, but selfishness divides. Therefore, "speaking the truth in love," let us equip one another and edify one another, that all of us may grow up to be more like Christ.

QUESTIONS FOR PERSONAL REFLECTION
OR GROUP DISCUSSION

1. What do you think are the main factors that contribute to the success of a sports team?

2. Read Ephesians 4:1–16 where Paul emphasized a major factor that contributes to the success of the church: unity. What is the "unity of the Spirit"? What is the basis for unity among believers?

3. Why is unity so important?

4. Why is disunity (squabbling, cliques, power struggles, sniping about other denominations) unworthy of our calling?

5. How does humility aid unity?

6. How do patience and bearing with one another aid unity?

7. What's the connection in this passage between unity and a diversity of gifts?

8. Paul says God gives leaders (apostles, prophets, etc.) to equip other believers to do works of service so that the whole body becomes united and mature. Are you equipped for works of service? If so, what services are you doing? If not, what equipping do you need?

9. What happens to the body of Christ if the leaders do all the works of service?

10. What evidences of spiritual growth does Paul mention?

11. How can you contribute to unity and maturity in the body of Christ?

Chapter Nine

TAKE OFF THE GRAVECLOTHES!

(Ephesians 4:17–32)

The Bible was written to be obeyed, and not simply studied, and this is why the words "therefore" and "wherefore" are repeated so often in the second half of Ephesians (4:1, 17, 25; 5:1, 7, 14, 17, 24). Paul was saying, "Here is what Christ has done for you. Now, in the light of this, here is what we ought to do for Christ." We are to be doers of the Word, and not hearers only (James 1:22). The fact that we have been called in Christ (Eph. 1:18) ought to motivate us to walk in unity (Eph. 4:1–16). And the fact that we have been raised from the dead (Eph. 2:1–10) should motivate us to walk in purity (Eph. 4:17—5:17), or, as Paul told the Romans, "walk in newness of life" (Rom. 6:4). We are alive in Christ, not dead in sins; therefore "put off the old man ... and put on the new man" (Eph. 4:22, 24). Take off the graveclothes and put on the grace-clothes!

THE ADMONITION (4:17–19)

There are some negatives in the Christian life, and here is one of them: "Walk not as other Gentiles walk." The Christian is not to imitate the life of the unsaved people around him. They are "dead in trespasses and sins" (Eph. 2:1), while he has been raised from the dead and been given eternal life in Christ. Paul explains the differences between the saved and the unsaved.

To begin with, Christians *think* differently from unsaved people. Note the emphasis here on thinking: mind (Eph. 4:17, 23), understanding (Eph. 4:18), ignorance (Eph. 4:18), "learned Christ" (Eph. 4:20). Salvation begins with repentance, which is a change of mind. The whole outlook of a person changes when he trusts Christ, including his values, goals, and interpretation of life. What is wrong with the mind of the unsaved person? For one thing, his thinking is "vain" (futile). It leads to no substantial purpose. Since he does not know God, he cannot truly understand the world around him, nor can he understand himself. The sad story is told in Romans 1:21–25. Our world today possesses a great deal of knowledge, but very little wisdom. Thoreau put it beautifully when he said that we have "improved means to unimproved ends."

The unsaved man's thinking is futile because it is darkened. He thinks he is enlightened because he rejects the Bible and believes the latest philosophies, when in reality he is in the dark. "Professing themselves to be wise, they became fools" (Rom. 1:22). But they think they are wise. Satan has blinded the minds of the unsaved (2 Cor. 4:3–6) because he does not want them to see the truth in Jesus Christ. It is not simply that their eyes are blinded so they cannot see, but that their minds are darkened so that they cannot think straight about spiritual matters.

Of course, the unsaved man is dead because of this spiritual ignorance. The truth and the life go together. If you believe God's truth, then you receive God's life. But you would think that the unbeliever would do his utmost to get out of his terrible spiritual plight. Alas, the hardness of his heart enslaves him. He is "past feeling" because he has so given himself over to sin that sin controls him. Read Romans 1:18–32 for a vivid expansion of these three brief verses.

The Christian cannot pattern himself after the unsaved person, because the Christian has experienced a miracle of being raised from the dead. His life is not futile, but purposeful. His mind is filled with the light of God's Word, and his heart with the fullness of God's life. He gives his body to God as an instrument of righteousness (Rom. 6:13), and not to sin for the satisfaction of his own selfish lusts. In every way, the believer is different from the unbeliever, and therefore the admonition: "Walk not."

THE ARGUMENT (4:20–24)

Paul reinforced his admonition with an argument from the spiritual experience of his readers. Again the emphasis is on the mind, or the outlook, of the believer. "But ye have not so learned Christ" (Eph. 4:20). He did not say "learned about Christ," because it is possible to learn about Christ and never be saved. To "learn Christ" means to have a personal relationship to Christ so that you get to know Him better each day. I can learn about Sir Winston Churchill because I own many of his books and can secure books about his life. But I can never "learn him" because he is dead. Jesus Christ is alive! Therefore, I can "learn Christ" through a personal fellowship with Him.

This fellowship is based on the Word of God. I can be taught "the truth" as it is in Jesus Christ. The better I understand the Word of God, the better I know the Son of God, for the whole Bible is a revelation of the Lord Jesus Christ (Luke 24:27; John 5:39). The unsaved man is spiritually ignorant, while the Christian is intelligent in the things of the Word. And the unsaved man does not know Christ, while the believer grows in his personal knowledge of Christ day by day. We have believed the truth; we have received the life; therefore, we will walk "in the way" and not walk after the example of the unsaved world.

But this experience of salvation goes much deeper than this, for it has resulted in a whole new position before God. The old man (the former life) has been put away, and we can now walk in newness of life through Christ. Ephesians 4:22–24 is a summary of Romans 5—8, where Paul explained the believer's identification with Christ in death, burial, and resurrection. He also dealt with this in Ephesians 2:4–6, as well as in Colossians 3. As Christians, we have not simply changed our minds. We have totally changed our citizenship. We belong to God's "new creation" in Christ (2 Cor. 5:17), and therefore, the ideas and desires of the old creation no longer should control our lives.

The simplest illustration of this great truth is given in John 11, the resurrection of Lazarus. Our Lord's friend, Lazarus, had been in the grave four days when Jesus and His disciples arrived at Bethany, and even Martha admitted that, by now, the decaying body would smell (John 11:39). But Jesus spoke the word and Lazarus came forth alive, an illustration of John 5:24. Notice our Lord's next words: "Loose him, and let him go" (John 11:44). Take off the graveclothes! Lazarus no longer belonged to the old dominion of death, for he was now alive. Why go about wearing graveclothes? Take off the old and put on the new!

This was Paul's argument—you no longer belong to the old corruption of sin; you belong to the new creation in Christ. Take off the graveclothes! How do we do this? "Be renewed in the spirit of your mind" (Eph. 4:23). Conversion is a crisis that leads to a process. Through Christ, once and for all, we have been given a new position in His new creation, but day by day, we must by faith appropriate what He has given us. The Word of God renews the mind as we surrender our all to Him (Rom. 12:1–2). "Sanctify them through thy truth: thy word is truth" (John 17:17). As the mind understands the truth of God's Word, it is gradually transformed by the Spirit, and this renewal leads to a changed life. Physically, you are what you eat, but spiritually, you are what you think. "As he thinketh in his heart, so is he" (Prov. 23:7). This is why it is important for us as Christians to spend time daily meditating on the Word, praying, and fellowshipping with Christ.

THE APPLICATION (4:25–32)

Paul was not content to explain a principle and then leave it. He always applied it to the different areas of life that need to feel its power. Paul even dared to name sins. Five different sins are named in this section, and Paul told us to avoid them and he explained why.

Lying (v. 25). A lie is a statement that is contrary to fact, spoken with the intent to deceive. If I tell you it is noon, and then discover that my watch is wrong, I did not tell a lie. But if I gave you the wrong time so you would be late to a meeting and I would benefit from it, that would be a lie. Satan is a liar (John 8:44), and he wants us to believe that God is a liar. "Yea, hath God said?" (Gen. 3:1). Whenever we speak truth, the Spirit of God works, but whenever we tell a lie, Satan goes to work. We like to believe that we help people by lying to them, but such is not the case. We may not see the sad consequences immediately, but ultimately they will come. "Ye know … that no lie is of the truth" (1 John 2:21). Hell is prepared for "whosoever loveth and maketh a lie" (Rev. 22:15). This does not mean that anybody who ever told a lie will go to hell, but rather that those whose lives are controlled by lies—they love lies and they make lies—are lost forever. The Christian's life is controlled by truth.

Note the reason Paul gave for telling the truth: We belong to each other in Christ. He urged us to build the body in love (Eph. 4:16) and he urged us to build the body in truth. "Speaking the truth in love" (Eph. 4:15). As "members one of another" we affect each other, and we cannot build each other apart from truth. The first sin that was judged in the early church was the sin of lying (Acts 5:1–11).

Anger (vv. 26–27). Anger is an emotional arousal caused by something that displeases us. In itself, anger is not a sin, because even God can be angry (Deut. 9:8, 20; Ps. 2:12). Several times in the Old Testament the phrase appears, "the anger of the Lord" (Num. 25:4; Jer. 4:8; 12:13). The holy anger of God is a part of His judgment against sin, as illustrated in our Lord's anger when He cleansed the temple (Matt. 21:12–13). The Bible often speaks of anger "being kindled" (Gen. 30:2; Deut. 6:15), as though anger can be compared to fire. Sometimes a man's anger smolders, and this we would call *malice,* but this same anger can suddenly burst forth and destroy, and this we would call *wrath.*

It is difficult for us to practice a truly holy anger or righteous indignation because our emotions are tainted by sin, and we do not have the same knowledge that God has in all matters. God sees everything clearly and knows everything completely, and we do not. The New Testament principle seems to be that the believer should be angry at sin but loving toward people. Compare this with the Old Testament: "Ye that love the LORD, hate evil" (Ps. 97:10).

It is possible to be angry and not sin, but if we do sin, we must settle the matter quickly and not let the sun go down on our wrath. "Agree with thine adversary quickly" (Matt. 5:25). "Go and tell him his fault between thee and him alone" (Matt. 18:15). The fire of anger, if not quenched by loving forgiveness, will spread and defile and destroy the work of God. According to Jesus, anger is the first step toward murder (Matt. 5:21–26), because anger gives the Devil a foothold in our lives, and Satan is a murderer (John 8:44). Satan hates God and God's people, and when he finds a believer with the sparks of anger in his heart, he fans those sparks, adds fuel to the fire, and does a great deal of damage to God's people and God's church. Both lying and anger "give place to the devil" (Eph. 4:27).

When I was living in Chicago, one out of every thirty-five deaths was a murder, and most of these murders involved relatives and friends. They are what the law calls "crimes of passion." Two friends get into an argument (often while gambling), one of them gets angry, pulls a gun or knife, and kills his friend. Horace was right when he said, "Anger is momentary insanity."

A woman tried to defend her bad temper by saying, "I explode and then it's all over with."

"Yes," replied a friend, "just like a shotgun—but look at the damage that's left behind."

"Anyone can become angry," wrote Aristotle. "But to be angry with the right person, to the right degree, at the right time, for the right purpose, and in the right way—this is not easy."

Solomon has a good solution: "A soft answer turneth away wrath: but grievous words stir up anger" (Prov. 15:1).

Stealing (v. 28). "Thou shalt not steal" is one of the Ten Commandments, and when God gave that commandment, He instituted the right of private ownership of property. A man has the right to turn his strength into gain, and to keep that gain and use it as he sees fit. God gave numerous laws to the Jews for the protection of their property, and these principles have become a part of our law today. Stealing was particularly a sin of the slaves in Paul's day. Usually they were not well cared for and were always in need, and the law gave them almost no protection. When he wrote to Titus, Paul urged him to admonish the slaves not to "purloin" but to be faithful to their masters (Titus 2:10). But it was not only the slaves, but citizens in general, who were addicted to thievery, for Paul wrote to people in the Ephesian church who were gainfully employed (Eph. 4:28).

Just as Satan is a liar and a murderer, he is also a thief. "The thief cometh not, but for to steal, and to kill, and to destroy" (John 10:10). He turned Judas into a thief (John 12:6), and he would do the same to us if he could. When he tempted Eve, he led her to become a thief, for she took the fruit that was forbidden. And she, in turn, made Adam a thief. The first Adam was a thief and was cast out of Paradise, but the Last Adam, Christ, turned to a thief and said, "Today shalt thou be with me in paradise" (Luke 23:43).

Paul added motive to the admonition. We should tell the truth because we are "members one of another." We should control our anger lest we "give place to the devil." We should work, and not steal, so that we might be able "to give to him that needeth." You would expect Paul to have said, "Let him work that he might take care of himself and not be tempted to steal." Instead, he lifted human labor to a much higher level. We work that we might be able to help others. If we steal, we hurt others; therefore, we should work that we might be able to help others. Even honest labor could become a selfish thing, and this Paul seeks to avoid. Of course, it was a fundamental rule in the early church that "if any would not work, neither should he eat" (2 Thess. 3:10). A lazy Christian robs himself, others, and God. Of course, Paul was not writing to believers who could not work because of handicaps, but with those who would not work.

Paul himself was an example of a hard worker, for while he was establishing local churches, he labored as a tentmaker. Every Jewish rabbi was taught a trade, for, said the rabbis, "If you do not teach your son a trade, you teach him to be a thief." The men that God called in the Scriptures were busy working when their call came. Moses was caring for sheep; Gideon was threshing wheat; David was minding his father's flock; and the first four disciples were either casting nets or mending them. Jesus Himself was a carpenter.

Corrupt speech (v. 29). The mouth and heart are connected. "Out of the abundance of the heart, the mouth speaketh" (Matt. 12:34). We expect a change in speech when a person becomes a Christian. It is interesting to trace the word *mouth* through the book of Romans and see how Christ makes a difference in a man's speech. The sinner's mouth is "full of cursing and bitterness" (Rom. 3:14), but when he trusts Christ, he gladly confesses with his mouth "Jesus Christ is Lord" (Rom. 10:9–10 NIV). As a condemned sinner, his mouth is stopped before the throne of God (Rom. 3:19), but as a believer, his mouth is opened to praise God (Rom. 15:6). Change the heart and you change the speech. Paul certainly knew the difference, for when he was an unsaved rabbi, he was "breathing out threatenings and slaughter against the disciples of the Lord" (Acts 9:1). But when he trusted Christ, a change took place: "Behold, he prayeth" (Acts 9:11). From "preying" to "praying" in one step of faith!

The word *corrupt,* used in Matthew 7:17–18, refers to rotten fruit. It means "that which is worthless, bad, or rotten." Our words do not have to be "dirty" to be worthless. Sometimes we go along with the crowd and try to impress people with the fact that we are not as puritanical as they think. Peter may have had this motive in mind when he was accused by the girl of being one of Christ's disciples. "Then began he to curse and to swear, saying, 'I know not the man'" (Matt. 26:74). The appetites of the old life sometimes show up when we permit "filthy communication" out of the mouth (Col. 3:8). Remember, before we were saved, we lived in spiritual death (Eph. 2:1–3), and, like Lazarus, our personal corruption produced an odor that was not pleasing to God. No wonder Paul wrote, "Their throat is an open sepulchre" (Rom. 3:13).

The remedy is to make sure the heart is full of blessing. So fill the heart with the love of Christ so that only truth and purity can come out of the mouth. Never have to say, "Now, take this with a grain of salt." Paul told us to put the salt of God's grace in everything we say. "Let your speech be always with grace, seasoned with salt" (Col. 4:6). And keep in mind that your words have power, either for good or evil. Paul told us to speak in such a way that what we say will build up our hearers, and not tear them down.

Our words should minister grace and help to draw others closer to Christ. Satan, of course, encourages speech that will tear people down and destroy the work of Christ. If you need to be reminded of the power of the tongue, read the third chapter of James.

Bitterness (vv. 30–32). These verses warn us against several sins of the attitude and amplify what Paul wrote about anger. *Bitterness* refers to a settled hostility that poisons the whole inner man. Somebody does something we do not like, so we harbor ill will against him. "Husbands, love your wives, and be not bitter against them" (Col. 3:19). Bitterness leads to wrath, which is the explosion on the outside of the feelings on the inside. Wrath and anger often lead to brawling (clamor) or blasphemy (evil speaking). The first is fighting with fists, the second is fighting with words. It is difficult to believe that Christians would act this way, but they do, and this is why Paul warned us. "Behold, how good and how pleasant it is for brethren to dwell together in unity!" (Ps. 133:1).

A handsome elderly man stopped at my study one day and asked me if I would perform a wedding for him. I suggested that he bring the bride in so that we might chat together and get better acquainted, since I hesitate to marry strangers. "Before she comes in," he said, "let me explain this wedding to you. Both of us have been married before—to each other! Over thirty years ago, we got into an argument, I got mad, and we separated. Then we did a stupid thing and got a divorce. I guess we were both too proud to apologize. Well, all these years we've lived alone, and now we see how foolish we've been. Our bitterness has robbed us of the joys of life, and now we want to remarry and see if the Lord won't give us a few years of happiness before we die." Bitterness and anger, usually over trivial things, make havoc of homes, churches, and friendships.

Paul gave three reasons why we must avoid bitterness. First, *it grieves the Holy Spirit.* He lives within the Christian, and when the heart is filled with bitterness and anger, the Spirit grieves. We parents know just a little of this feeling when our children at home fight with each other. The Holy Spirit is happiest in an atmosphere of love, joy, and peace, for these are the "fruit of the Spirit" that He produces in our lives as we obey Him. The Holy Spirit cannot leave us, because He has sealed us until that day when Christ returns to take us home. We do not lose our salvation because of our sinful attitudes, but we certainly lose the joy of our salvation and the fullness of the Spirit's blessing.

Second, our sin *grieves God the Son*, who died for us. Third, it *grieves God the Father*, who forgave us when we trusted Christ. Here Paul put his finger on the basic cause of a bitter attitude: We cannot forgive people. An unforgiving spirit is the Devil's playground, and before long it becomes the Christian's battleground. If somebody hurts us, either deliberately or unintentionally, and we do not forgive him, then we begin to develop bitterness within, which hardens the heart. We should be tenderhearted and kind, but instead we are hardhearted and bitter. Actually, we are not hurting the person who hurt us; we are only hurting ourselves. Bitterness in the heart makes us treat others the way Satan treats them, when we should treat others the way God has treated us. In His gracious kindness, God has forgiven us, and we should forgive others. We do not forgive for *our* sake (though we do get a blessing from it) or even for *their* sake, but for *Jesus'* sake. Learning how to forgive and forget is one of the secrets of a happy Christian life.

Review once again the motives for "walking in purity": We are members one of another; Satan wants to get a foothold in our lives; we ought to share with others; we ought to build one another up; and we ought not to grieve God. And, after all, we have been raised from the dead—so why wear the graveclothes? Jesus says of us as He said of Lazarus: "Loose him, and let him go!"

QUESTIONS FOR PERSONAL REFLECTION
OR GROUP DISCUSSION

1. What do you do with things when they become old?

2. Read Ephesians 4:17–32. How did Paul compare the old, or unsaved, man with the new, or saved?

3. How does this description compare with his previous descriptions of unsaved and saved people in Ephesians 2:1–9?

4. Why should believers live differently than they did before they were saved?

5. Look at the sins that Paul specifically names in verses 25–32 that we are to get rid of. How does each of these sins undermine the body of Christ?

6. Which of these sins is the greatest temptation for you? How so?

7. How do we grieve the Holy Spirit?

8. What should be our motives for putting "on the new man"?

9. What old sins have you discarded since you became a Christian?

10. How can you "put off" the old man and "put on" the new man?

Chapter Ten

IMITATING OUR FATHER

(Ephesians 5:1–17)

T he word *followers* in Ephesians 5:1 is the word *mimics,* so that the verse can be translated "Be ye imitators of God as beloved children." This sets the theme for the section. Paul was simply arguing that children are like their parents, a fact that can be both encouraging and embarrassing to those of us who have children. Have you ever seen a child sitting in the front seat of an automobile, trying to drive like his father? Or walking behind him, pretending to mow the lawn? Or, sad to say, imitating Dad smoking a cigarette or taking a drink of alcohol? Children probably learn more by watching and imitating than any other way.

If we are the children of God, then we ought to imitate our Father. This is the basis for the three admonitions in this section. God is love (1 John 4:8); therefore, "walk in love" (Eph. 5:1–2). God is light (1 John 1:5); therefore, "walk as children of light" (Eph. 5:3–14). God is truth (1 John 5:6); therefore, walk in wisdom (Eph. 5:15–17). Of course, each of these "walks" is a part of Paul's exhortation to "walk in purity."

1. WALK IN LOVE (5:1–2)

This admonition ties in with the last two verses of the previous chapter where Paul has warned us against bitterness and anger. It is tragic when these attitudes show up in the family of God. As a pastor, I have witnessed malice and bitterness in the lives of people as I have conducted funerals and even weddings. You would think that sharing the sorrow of losing a loved one, or sharing a joy of a marriage, would enable people to forgive past wrongs and try to get along with each other. But such is not the case. It takes a real love in the heart, for "charity [love] shall cover the multitude of sins" (1 Peter 4:8).

Paul gave several reasons why the Christian ought to walk in love.

He is God's child. Having been born again through faith in Christ, he is therefore one of the "partakers of the divine nature" (2 Peter 1:4), and since "God is love" it is logical that God's children will walk in love. When Paul encouraged his readers to "walk in love," he was not asking them to do something that was foreign to the Christian life; for we have received a new nature that wants to express itself in love. The old nature is basically selfish, and for this reason builds walls and declares war. But the new nature is loving, and therefore builds bridges and proclaims peace.

He is God's beloved child. "Be ye imitators of God as beloved children." Imagine, God speaks of us the same way He spoke of Jesus Christ: "This is my beloved Son" (Matt. 3:17). In fact, the Father loves us as He loves His Son (John 17:23). We are born into a loving relationship with the Father that ought to result in our showing love to Him by the way we live. What more could the Father do to express His love to us? Is it asking too much for us to "walk in love" to please Him?

He was purchased with a great price. "Greater love hath no man than this, that a man lay down his life for his friends" (John 15:13). But He laid down His life for His enemies (Rom. 5:10). Our love for Him is our response to His love for us. Paul compared Christ's sacrifice on the cross to the Old Testament "sweet savor" sacrifices that were presented at the altar of the temple (Lev. 1:9, 13, 17; 2:9). The idea behind "sweet savor" is simply that the sacrifice is well pleasing to God. This does not suggest that God is pleased that sin demands death, and that His Son had to die to save lost sinners. Rather, it indicates that the death of Christ satisfies the holy law of God and therefore is acceptable and pleasing to the Father. The sweet-savor offerings are described in Leviticus 1–3: the burnt offering, the meal offering, and the peace offering. The burnt offering pictures Christ's complete devotion to God; the meal offering, His perfection of character; and the peace offering, His making peace between sinners and God. Since the sin offering and the trespass offering (Lev. 4—5) picture Christ taking the place of the sinner, they are not considered "sweet-savor" offerings. Certainly nothing is beautiful about sin!

Paul began with "walk in love" because love is the fundamental factor in the Christian life. If we walk in love, we will not disobey God or injure men because "he that loveth another hath fulfilled the law" (Rom. 13:8). The Holy Spirit puts this love in our hearts (Rom. 5:5).

2. WALK AS CHILDREN OF LIGHT (5:3–14)

Since "God is light" and we are imitating our Father, then we should walk in the light and have nothing to do with the darkness of sin. Paul gave three descriptions of believers that prove his point.

We are saints (vv. 3–4). That is, we are "set-apart ones" and no longer belong to the world of darkness around us. We have been "called out of darkness into his marvelous light" (1 Peter 2:9). It is beneath the dignity of a saint to indulge in the sins that belong to the world of darkness, some of which Paul named here. He warned us against the sexual sins (fornication, uncleanness) that were so prevalent in that day—and are prevalent today. Sad to say, these sins have invaded the homes of Christians and brought grief to local churches too. "Covetousness" may seem out of place next to fornication, but the two sins are but different expressions of the same basic weakness of fallen nature—uncontrolled appetite. The fornicator and the covetous person each desire to satisfy the appetite by taking what does not belong to them. "The lust of the flesh, and the lust of the eyes" (1 John 2:16) would describe these two sins. "Let there not be even a hint of these sins!" said Paul.

In Ephesians 5:4 he warned against sins of the tongue, which, of course, are really sins of the heart. It is not difficult to see the relationship between the sins named in Ephesians 5:3 and those in Ephesians 5:4. People who have base appetites usually cultivate a base kind of speech and humor, and often people who want to commit sexual sins, or have committed them, enjoy jesting about them. Two indications of a person's character are what makes him laugh and what makes him weep. The saint of God sees nothing humorous in obscene language or jests. "Foolish talking" does not mean innocent humor but rather senseless conversation that cheapens the man and does not edify or minister grace to the hearers (Eph. 4:29). Paul was not condemning small talk because much conversation falls into that classification. He was condemning foolish talk that accomplishes no good purpose.

Jesting is a translation of a word that means "able to turn easily." This suggests a certain kind of conversationalist who can turn any statement into a coarse jest. The gift of wit is a blessing, but when it is attached to a filthy mind or a base motive, it becomes a curse. There are quick-witted people who can pollute any conversation with jests that are always inconvenient (out of place). How much better it is for us to be quick to give thanks! This is certainly the best way to give glory to God and keep the conversation pure.

A Christian woman attended an anniversary dinner in honor of a friend, not knowing that there would be a program of low comedy following the meal. The so-called comedian tried to entertain the crowd with coarse humor that degraded everything that the Christian guest held to be sacred and honorable. At one point in the program, the comedian's throat became dry. "Please bring me a glass of water," he called to a waiter.

At that point the Christian woman added, "And bring a toothbrush and a bar of soap with it!" To be sure, soap in the mouth will never cleanse the conversation, but she made her point.

Christians who have God's Word in their hearts (Col. 3:16) will always season their speech with salt (Col. 4:6), for grace in the heart means grace on the lips.

We are kings (vv. 5–6). When we trusted Christ, we entered into the kingdom of God (John 3:3), but we are also awaiting the full revelation of His kingdom when He returns (2 Tim. 4:1). Paul made it clear that people who deliberately and persistently live in sin will not share in God's kingdom. "They which practice such things shall not inherit the kingdom of God" (Gal. 5:21, literal translation). "Whoremonger" is a translation of the Greek word *pornos,* from which we get our word *pornography,* and it means "one who practices fornication—illicit sex." The morally unclean and the covetous will join the fornicator in judgment. Paul equated covetousness with idolatry, for it is the worship of something other than God. These warnings deal with the habitual practice of sin, and not the occasional act of sin. David committed adultery, yet God forgave him and one day took him to heaven. Certainly David was disciplined for his sin, but he was not rejected by God.

In Paul's day, there were false Christians who argued that believers could live in sin and get away with it. These deceivers had many arguments to convince ignorant Christians that they could sin repeatedly and still enter God's kingdom. "You were saved by grace!" they argued. "Therefore go ahead and sin that God's grace might abound!" Paul answered that foolish argument in Romans 6. "Sin in the life of a believer is different from sin in the life of an unsaved person!" Yes—*it's worse!* God judges sin no matter where He finds it, and He does not want to find it in the life of one of His own children. I personally believe that no true Christian can ever be lost, but he will prove the reality of his faith by an obedient life.

There are many professors who are not possessors (Matt. 7:21–23). A Christian is not *sinless,* but he does *sin less*—and less—and less! The Christian is a king, and it is beneath his dignity to indulge in the practices of the lost world that is outside the kingdom of God.

We are light (vv. 7–14). This figure is the main thrust of the passage, for Paul was admonishing his readers to "walk as children of light." You will want to read 2 Corinthians 6:14—7:1 for a parallel passage that explains the contrasts that exist between the child of God and the unsaved person. Paul did not say that we were "in the darkness," but that we "were darkness." Now that we are saved, "what communion hath light with darkness?" After all, light produces fruit, but the works of darkness are unfruitful as far as spiritual things are concerned. "For the fruit of the Spirit [or "the light"] is in all goodness and righteousness and truth." It is impossible to be in darkness and light at the same time!

The light produces "goodness," one manifestation of the fruit of the Spirit (Gal. 5:22). Goodness is "love in action." Righteousness means rightness of character before God and rightness of actions before men. Both of these qualities are based on *truth,* which is conformity to the Word and will of God.

Jesus had much to say about light and darkness. "Let your light so shine before men, that they may see your good works, and glorify your Father which is in heaven" (Matt. 5:16). "Every one that doeth evil hateth the light, neither cometh to the light, lest his deeds should be reproved. But he that doeth truth cometh to the light, that his deeds may be made manifest, that they are wrought in God" (John 3:20–21).

To "walk as children of light" means to live before the eyes of God, not hiding anything. It is relatively easy to hide things from other people because they cannot see our hearts and minds, but "all things are naked and opened unto the eyes of him with whom we have to do" (Heb. 4:13). Every time I take a plane to a meeting, I must surrender myself and my luggage to a special inspection, and I am happy to do so, because this inspection helps to detect bombs. I have never been afraid to walk through the "detection tunnel" or have my luggage pass through the X-ray equipment, because I have nothing to hide.

An author asked Charles Spurgeon for permission to write his life story, and the great preacher replied, "You may write my life in the skies—I have nothing to hide!"

But walking "as children of light" also means revealing God's light in our daily lives. By our character and conduct, we bring God's light into a dark world. As God's lights, we help others find their way to Christ. The mind of the unsaved person is blinded by Satan (2 Cor. 4:3–4) and by sin (Eph. 4:17–19). Only as we witness and share Christ can the light enter in. Just as a healthy person can assist the sickly, so a child of God can lead the lost out of darkness into God's wonderful light.

Light reveals God; light produces fruit; but light also exposes what is wrong. No surgeon would willingly operate in darkness lest he make a false move and take a life. How could an artist paint a true picture in darkness? The light reveals the truth and exposes the true character of things. This explains why the unsaved person stays clear of the church and the Bible. God's light reveals his true character, and the exposure is not very complimentary. As we Christians walk in light, we refuse to fellowship with the darkness, and we expose the dark things of sin for what they really are.

"I am come a light into the world," said Jesus (John 12:46). He also said to His disciples, "Ye are the light of the world" (Matt. 5:14). When

He was here on earth, the perfection of His character and conduct exposed the sinfulness of those around Him. This is one reason why the religious leaders hated Him and sought to destroy Him. "If I had not come and spoken unto them, they had not had sin: but now they have no cloak for their sin" (John 15:22). Just as a healthy person unconsciously exposes the handicaps and sicknesses of people he visits in a hospital, so the Christian exposes the darkness and sin around him just by living like a Christian. Paul told us to live balanced lives—positively, to walk in the light; negatively, to denounce and expose the wickedness of those in the darkness. It is not enough simply to expose the wickedness of those in the darkness. It is not enough simply to expose sin. We must also bear fruit.

But Ephesians 5:12 gives us a caution. Be careful how you deal with the "unfruitful works of darkness." The motto today seems to be "Tell it like it is!" And yet that can be a dangerous policy when it comes to exposing the filthy things of darkness, lest we unconsciously advertise and promote sin. Paul said, "It is a shame even to speak of those things" (Eph. 5:12). Some preachers enjoy reveling in the sensational, so much so that their sermons excite appetites and give to the innocent more information than they need. "But yet I would have you wise unto that which is good, and simple concerning evil" (Rom. 16:19).

I recall a friend in youth work who felt it necessary to read all that the teenagers were reading "in order to understand them better," and it so polluted his mind that he himself fell into sin. It is not necessary for the believer to perform an autopsy on a rotting corpse to expose its rottenness. All he has to do is turn on the light! "For whatsoever doth make manifest is light" (Eph. 5:13).

When you think of light, you think of waking up to a new day, and Paul presented this picture (Eph. 5:14), paraphrasing Isaiah 60:1. You have the same image in Romans 13:11–13 and 1 Thessalonians 5:1–10. That Easter morning, when Christ arose from the dead, was the dawning of a new day for the world. Christians are not sleeping in sin and death. We have been raised from the dead through faith in Him. The darkness of the graveyard is past, and we are now walking in the light of salvation. Salvation is the beginning of a new day, and we ought to live as those who belong to the light, not to the darkness. "Lazarus, come forth!"

The believer has no business in the darkness. He is a *saint,* which means he is a partaker "of the inheritance of the saints in light" (Col. 1:12). He is a *king,* because he has been delivered "from the power of darkness" and has been translated "into the kingdom of his dear Son" (Col. 1:13). He is "light in the Lord" (Eph. 5:8).

3. WALK IN WISDOM (5:15–17)

Circumspect comes from two Latin words that mean "looking around." The Greek word carries the idea of precision and accuracy. "See that you walk carefully, with exactness" is the meaning. The opposite would be walking carelessly and without proper guidance and forethought. We cannot leave the Christian life to chance. We must make wise decisions and seek to do the will of God.

Ephesians 5:14–15 are related to these verses. Paul appeared to be saying, "Don't walk in your sleep! Wake up! Open your eyes! Make the most of the day!" It is sad to see many professed Christians drift through life like sleepwalkers, never really making the most of opportunities to live for Christ and serve Him. Paul presented several reasons why we should be accurate and careful in our walk.

It is a mark of wisdom (v. 15). Only a fool drifts with the wind and tide. A wise man marks out his course, sets his sails, and guides the rudder until he reaches his destination. When a man wants to build a house, he first draws his plans so he knows what he is doing. Yet, how many Christians plan their days so that they use their opportunities wisely? True, we cannot know what a day may bring forth (James 4:13–17). But it is also true that a planned life can better deal with unexpected events. Someone said, "When the pilot does not know what port he is heading for, no wind is the right wind."

Life is short (v. 16a). "Buying up the opportunity—taking advantage of it." An old Chinese adage says, "Opportunity has a forelock so you can seize it when you meet it. Once it is past, you cannot seize it again." Our English word *opportunity* comes from the Latin and means "toward the port." It suggests a ship taking advantage of the wind and tide to arrive safely in the harbor. The brevity of life is a strong argument for making the best use of the opportunities God gives us.

The days are evil (v. 16b). In Paul's time, this meant that Roman persecution was on the way (1 Peter 4:12–19). How foolish to waste opportunities to win the lost, when soon those opportunities might be taken away by the advances of sin in society! If the days were evil when Paul wrote this letter, what must be their condition today?

God has given us a mind (v. 17a). "Understanding" suggests using our minds to discover and do the will of God. Too many Christians have the idea that discovering God's will is a mystical experience that rules out clear thinking. But this idea is wrong—and dangerous. We discover the will of God as He transforms the mind (Rom. 12:1–2); and this transformation is the result of the Word of God, prayer, meditation, and worship. If God gave you a mind, then He expects you to use it. This means that learning His will involves gathering facts, examining them, weighing them, and praying for His wisdom (James 1:5). God does not want us simply to *know* His will; He wants us to *understand* His will.

God has a plan for our lives (v. 17b). Paul alluded to this plan (Eph. 2:10). If God saved me, He has a purpose for my life, and I should discover that purpose and then guide my life accordingly. He reveals His plan through His Word (Col. 1:9–10), His Spirit in our hearts (Col. 3:15), and the working of circumstances (Rom. 8:28). The Christian can walk carefully and accurately because he knows what God wants him to do. Like the builder following the blueprint, he accomplishes what the architect planned.

This completes the section we have called "Walk in Purity." The emphasis is on the new life as contrasted with the old life, imitating God and not the evil world around us. In the next section, "Walk in Harmony," Paul deals with the relationships of life and shows how life in Christ can bring heaven to the home.

QUESTIONS FOR PERSONAL REFLECTION
OR GROUP DISCUSSION

1. What are some ways a child imitates his or her parents?

2. Read Ephesians 5:1–17. In this passage, Paul writes about three ways believers can imitate their heavenly Father: Walk in love, light, and wisdom. How have you experienced God as love? As light? As wisdom?

3. What are some practical ways we can imitate God's love?

4. How did Paul describe our walk as children of light?

5. What are some contemporary ways of doing that?

6. Most of us know that sexual immorality is walking in darkness. But why does Paul equate greed with idolatry?

7. In what ways does our society tempt us to walk in the darkness of greed?

8. Why is it important for believers to walk in wisdom?

9. Specifically how can we walk, or live, wisely?

10. How are these three walks related to our walk in purity, the theme of 4:17—5:17?

11. Which of these three walks do you most need to concentrate on in your spiritual life? How will you practice it?

Chapter Eleven

HEAVEN IN YOUR HOME
(Ephesians 5:18–33)

W hen home is ruled according to God's Word," said Charles Haddon Spurgeon, "angels might be asked to stay with us, and they would not find themselves out of their element."

The trouble is that many homes are not governed by God's Word—even homes where the members are professing Christians—and the consequences are tragic. Instead of angels being guests in some homes, it seems that demons are the masters. Too many marriages end in the divorce court, and nobody knows how many husbands and wives are emotionally divorced even though they share the same address. The poet William Cowper called the home "the only bliss of Paradise that hast surviv'd the Fall," but too many homes are an outpost of hell instead of a parcel of paradise.

The answer is the Holy Spirit of God! It is only through the power of the Holy Spirit that we can walk in harmony as husbands and wives (Eph. 5:22–33), parents and children (Eph. 6:1–4), and employers and employees (Eph. 6:5–9). The unity of the people of God that Paul described (Eph. 4:1–16) must be translated into daily living if we are to enjoy the harmony that is a foretaste of heaven on earth.

"Be filled with the Spirit" is God's command, and He expects us to obey. The command is plural, so it applies to all Christians and not just to a select few. The verb is in the present tense—"keep on being filled"—so it is an experience we should enjoy constantly and not just on special occasions. And the verb is passive. We do not fill ourselves but permit the Spirit to fill us. The verb "fill" has nothing to do with contents or quantity, as though we are empty vessels that need a required amount of spiritual fuel to keep going. In the Bible, *filled* means "controlled by." "They … were filled with wrath" (Luke 4:28) means "they were controlled by wrath" and for that reason tried to kill Jesus. "The Jews … were filled with envy" (Acts 13:45) means that the Jews were controlled by envy and opposed the ministry of Paul and Barnabas. To be "filled with the Spirit" means to be constantly controlled by the Spirit in our mind, emotions, and will.

When a person trusts Christ as his Savior, he is immediately baptized by the Spirit into the body of Christ (1 Cor. 12:13). Nowhere in the New Testament are we commanded to be baptized by the Spirit, because this is a once-for-all experience that takes place at conversion. When the Spirit came at Pentecost, the believers were baptized by the Spirit, and thus the body of Christ was formed (Acts 1:4–5). But they were also "filled with the Spirit" (Acts 2:4), and it was this filling that gave them the power they needed to witness for Christ (Acts 1:8). In Acts 2, the Jewish believers were baptized by the Spirit, and in Acts 10 the Gentile believers had the same experience (Acts 10:44–48; 11:15–17). Thus the body of Christ was made up of Jews and Gentiles (Eph. 2:11–22). That historic baptism, in two stages, has never been repeated any more than Calvary has been repeated. But that baptism is made personal when the sinner trusts Christ and the Spirit enters in to make him a member of the body of Christ. The baptism of the Spirit means that I belong to Christ's body. The filling of the Spirit means that my body belongs to Christ.

We usually think of the power of the Spirit as necessary for preaching and witnessing, and this is true. (See Acts 4:8, 31; 6:3, 5; 7:55; 13:9. The apostles experienced repeated fillings after that initial experience at Pentecost.) But Paul wrote that the Spirit's fullness is also needed in the home. If our homes are to be a heaven on earth, then we must be controlled by the Holy Spirit. But how can a person tell whether or not he is filled with the Spirit? Paul stated that there are three evidences of the fullness of the Spirit in the life of the believer: he is *joyful* (Eph. 5:19), *thankful* (Eph. 5:20), and *submissive* (Eph. 5:21–33). Paul said nothing about miracles or tongues or other special manifestations. He stated that the home can be a heaven on earth if each family member is controlled by the Spirit and is joyful, thankful, and submissive.

JOYFUL (5:19)

Joy is one of the fruits of the Spirit (Gal. 5:22). Christian joy is not a shallow emotion that, like a thermometer, rises and falls with the changing atmosphere of the home. Rather, Christian joy is a deep experience of adequacy and confidence in spite of the circumstances around us. The Christian can be joyful even in the midst of pain and suffering. This kind of joy is not a thermometer but a thermostat. Instead of rising and falling with the circumstances, it determines the spiritual temperature of the circumstances. Paul put it beautifully when he wrote, "I have learned, in whatsoever state I am, therewith to be content" (Phil. 4:11).

To illustrate this joy, Paul used the familiar image of drunkenness: "Be not drunk with wine ... but be filled with the Spirit" (Eph. 5:18). When the believers at Pentecost were filled with the Spirit, the crowd accused them of being drunk with new wine (Acts 2:13–15). There was such a joyfulness about them that the unbelievers could think of no better comparison. But some practical lessons can be learned from the contrasts. To begin with, the drunk is under the control of another force, since alcohol is actually a depressant. He feels a great sense of release—all his troubles are gone. He can "lick anybody in the house!" The drunk is not ashamed to express himself (though what he says and does is shameful), nor can he hide what is going on in his life.

Transfer this picture to the believer who is filled with the Spirit. God controls his life, and he experiences a deep joy he is not afraid to express to the glory of God. Of course, the drunk is really out of control, since the alcohol affects his brain, while the believer experiences a beautiful self-control that is really God in control. Self-control is among the fruit of the Spirit (Gal. 5:23). "The spirits of the prophets are subject to the prophets" (1 Cor. 14:32). The drunk makes a fool of himself, but the Spirit-filled Christian glorifies God and is willing to be a "fool for Christ's sake" (1 Cor. 4:10). The drunk calls attention to himself, while the Spirit-filled believer is a witness for Christ.

It is certainly not difficult to live or work with someone who is filled with the Spirit and joyful. He has a song in his heart and on his lips. The drunk often sings, but his songs only reveal the corruption in his heart. The Spirit-filled Christian's song comes from God, a song he could never sing apart from the Spirit's power. God even gives us songs in the night (Ps. 42:8). In spite of pain and shame, Paul and Silas were able to sing praises to God in the Philippian jail (Acts 16:25), and the result was the conversion of the jailer and his family. What a happy time they all had that midnight hour—and they did not need to get drunk to enjoy it!

"Your neighborhood tavern is the friendliest place in town!" That slogan appeared in a headline of a special newspaper insert during "National Tavern Month," so I decided to test its veracity. I watched the newspapers for several weeks and cut out items that related to taverns—and all of them were connected with brawls and murders. The friendliest place in town!

But this headline reminded me that people who drink together often experience a sympathy and conviviality. This fact is no argument for alcohol, but it does illustrate a point: Christians who are filled with the Holy Spirit enjoy being together and experience a sense of joyful oneness in the Lord. They do not need the false stimulants of the world. They have the Spirit of God—and He is all they need.

THANKFUL (5:20)

Someone defined the home as "the place where we are treated the best—and complain the most!" How true this is! "My father never talks to me unless he wants to bawl me out or ask about my grades," a teenager once told me. "After all, a guy needs some encouragement once in a while!" Marriage counselors tell us that "taking each other for granted" is one of the chief causes of marital problems. Being thankful to God for each other is a secret of a happy home, and it is the Holy Spirit who gives us the grace of thankfulness.

How does a grateful heart promote harmony in the home? For one thing, the sincerely grateful person realizes that he is enriched because of others, which is a mark of humility. The person who thinks the world owes him a living is never thankful for anything. He thinks he is doing others a favor by permitting them to serve him. The thankful heart is usually humble, a heart that gladly acknowledges God as the "Giver of every good and perfect gift" (James 1:17). Like Mary's gift to Jesus in John 12, gratitude fills the house with fragrance.

To be sure, all of us are grateful for some things at some special occasions, but Paul commanded his readers to be thankful for all things at all times. This exhortation in itself proves our need of the Spirit of God, because in our own strength we could never obey this commandment. Can we really be thankful in times of suffering, disappointment, and even bereavement? Keep in mind that Paul was a prisoner when he wrote those words, yet he was thankful for what God was doing in him and for him (Eph. 1:16; 5:4, 20; Phil. 1:3; Col. 1:3, 12; 2:7; 3:17; 4:2). When a Christian finds himself in a difficult situation, he should immediately give thanks to the Father, in the name of Jesus Christ, by the power of the Spirit, to keep his heart from complaining and fretting. The Devil moves in when a Christian starts to complain, but thanksgiving in the Spirit defeats the Devil and glorifies the Lord. "In every thing give thanks: for this is the will of God in Christ Jesus concerning you" (1 Thess. 5:18).

The word *gratitude* comes from the same root word as *grace*. If we have experienced the grace of God, then we ought to be grateful for what God brings to us. *Thank* and *think* also come from the same root word. If we would think more, we would thank more.

SUBMISSIVE (5:21–33)

Paul applied the principle of harmony to husbands and wives (Eph. 5:21–33), parents and children (Eph. 6:1–4), and masters and servants (Eph. 6:5–9), and he began with the admonition that each submit to the other (Eph. 5:21). Does this suggest that the children tell the parents what to do, or that the masters obey the servants? Of course not! *Submission* has nothing to do with the *order* of authority, but rather governs the *operation* of authority, how it is given and how it is received. Often Jesus tried to teach His disciples not to throw their weight around, or seek to become great at somebody else's expense. Unfortunately, they failed to learn the lesson, and even at the Last Supper they were arguing over who was the greatest (Luke 22:24–27). When Jesus washed their feet, He taught them that the greatest is the person who uses his authority to build up people and not, like the Pharisees, to build up his authority and make himself important. We are to esteem others "more important than ourselves"

(Rom. 12:10; Phil. 2:1–4). By nature, we want to promote ourselves, but the Holy Spirit enables us to submit ourselves.

As you study Paul's words to husbands and wives, remember that he was writing to believers. He was nowhere suggesting that women are inferior to men, or that all women must be in subjection to all men in every situation. The fact that he uses Christ and the church as his illustration is evidence that he has the Christian home in mind.

Wives, submit yourselves (vv. 22–24). He gives two reasons for this command: the lordship of Christ (Eph. 5:22) and the headship of the man in Christ (Eph. 5:23). When the Christian wife submits herself to Christ and lets Him be the Lord of her life, she will have no difficulty submitting to her husband. This does not mean that she becomes a slave, for the husband is also to submit to Christ. And if both are living under the lordship of Christ, there can be only harmony. Headship is not dictatorship. "Each for the other, both for the Lord." The Christian husband and wife should pray together and spend time in the Word, so that they might know God's will for their individual lives and for their home. Most of the marital conflicts I have dealt with as a pastor have stemmed from failure of the husband and/or wife to submit to Christ, spend time in His Word, and seek to do His will each day.

This explains why a Christian should marry a Christian and not become "unequally yoked together" with an unbeliever (2 Cor. 6:14–18). If the Christian is submitted to Christ, he will not try to establish a home that disobeys the Word of God. Such a home invites civil war from the beginning. But something else is important. The Christian couple must be careful to submit to Christ's lordship even before they are married. Unless the couple prays together and sincerely seeks God's will in His Word, their marriage begins on a weak foundation. Sins committed before marriage ("We're Christians—we can get away with this!") have a way of causing problems after marriage. Certainly God is able to forgive, but something very precious is lost just the same. Dr. William Culbertson, former president of Moody Bible Institute, used to warn about "the sad consequences of forgiven sins," and engaged Christian couples need to take that warning to heart.

Husbands, love your wives (vv. 25–33). Paul had much more to say to the Christian husbands than to the wives. He set for them a very high standard: Love your wives "even as Christ also loved the church." Paul was lifting married love to the highest level possible, for he saw in the Christian home an illustration of the relationship between Christ and the church. God established marriage for many reasons. For one thing, it meets man's *emotional* needs. "It is not good that the man should be alone" (Gen. 2:18). Marriage also has a *social* purpose in the bearing of children to continue the race (Gen. 1:28). Paul indicated a *physical* purpose for marriage—to help man and woman fulfill the normal desires given them by God (1 Cor. 7:1–3). But in Ephesians 5, Paul indicated also a *spiritual* purpose in marriage, as the husband and wife experience with each other the submission and the love of Christ (Eph. 5:22–33).

If the husband makes Christ's love for the church the pattern for loving his wife, then he will love her *sacrificially* (Eph. 5:25). Christ gave Himself for the church, so the husband, in love, gives himself for his wife. Jacob so loved Rachel that he sacrificially worked fourteen years to win her. True Christian love "seeketh not her own" (1 Cor. 13:5)—it is not selfish. If a husband is submitted to Christ and filled with the Spirit, his sacrificial love will willingly pay a price that she might be able to serve Christ in the home and glorify Him.

The husband's love will also be a *sanctifying* love (Eph. 5:26–27). The word *sanctify* means "to set apart." In the marriage ceremony, the husband is set apart to belong to the wife, and the wife is set apart to belong to the husband. Any interference with this God-given arrangement is sin. Today, Christ is cleansing His church through the ministry of His Word (John 15:3; 17:17). The love of the husband for his wife ought to be cleansing her (and him) so that both are becoming more like Christ. Even their physical relationship should be so controlled by God that it becomes a means of spiritual enrichment as well as personal enjoyment (1 Cor. 7:3–5). The husband is not to "use" his wife for his own pleasure, but rather is to show the kind of love that is mutually rewarding and sanctifying. The marriage experience is one of constant growth when Christ is the Lord of the home. Love always enlarges and enriches, while selfishness does just the opposite.

The church today is not perfect; it has spots and wrinkles. Spots are caused by defilement on the outside, while wrinkles are caused by decay on the inside. Because the church becomes defiled by the world, it needs constant cleansing, and the Word of God is the cleansing agent. "Keep yourselves unspotted from the world" (James 1:27). Strictly speaking, there should be no wrinkles in the church, because wrinkles are evidence of old age and internal decay. As the church is nourished by the Word, these wrinkles ought to disappear. Like a beautiful bride, the church ought to be clean and youthful, which is possible through the Spirit of God using the Word of God. One day the church will be presented in heaven "a glorious church" at the coming of Jesus Christ (Jude 24).

The husband's love for his wife should be sacrificial and sanctifying, but it should also be *satisfying* (Eph. 5:28–30). In the marriage relationship, the husband and wife become "one flesh." Therefore, whatever each does to the other, he or she does to himself or herself. It is a mutually satisfying experience. The man who loves his wife is actually loving his own body, since he and his wife are one flesh. As he loves her, he is nourishing her. Just as love is the circulatory system of the body of Christ (Eph. 4:16), so love is the nourishment of the home. How many people have confessed, "I am starved for love." There should be no starvation for love in the Christian home, for the husband and wife should so love each other that their physical, emotional, and spiritual needs are met. If both are submitted to the Lord, and to each other, they will be so satisfied that they will not be tempted to look anywhere else for fulfillment.

Our Christian homes are to be pictures of Christ's relationship to His church. Each believer is a member of Christ's body, and each believer is to help nourish the body in love (Eph. 4:16). We are one with Christ. The church is His body and His bride, and the Christian home is a divinely ordained illustration of this relationship. This certainly makes marriage a serious matter.

Paul referred to the creation of Eve and the forming of the first home (Gen. 2:18–24). Adam had to give part of himself in order to get a bride, but Christ gave all of Himself to purchase His bride at the cross. God opened Adam's side, but sinful men pierced Christ's side. So united are a husband and wife that they are "one flesh." Their union is even closer than that of parents and children. The believer's union with Christ is even closer and, unlike human marriage, will last for all eternity. Paul closed with a final admonition that the husband love his wife and that the wife reverence (respect) her husband, both of which require the power of the Holy Spirit.

If Christian husbands and wives have the power of the Spirit to enable them, and the example of Christ to encourage them, why do too many Christian marriages fail? Somebody is out of the will of God. Just because two Christians know each other and get along together does not mean they are supposed to get married. In fact, not every believer is supposed to marry. It is sometimes God's will for a Christian to remain single (Matt. 19:12; 1 Cor. 7:7–9). It is wrong for a believer to marry an unbeliever, but it is also wrong for two Christians to marry out of the will of God.

But even if two Christians marry in the will of God, they must stay in God's will if their home is to be the creative fellowship God wants it to be. "The fruit of the Spirit is love" (Gal. 5:22), and unless both husband and wife are walking in the Spirit they cannot share the love of Christ, the love that is so beautifully described in 1 Corinthians 13. The root of most marital problems is sin, and the root of all sin is selfishness. Submission to Christ and to one another is the only way to overcome selfishness, for when we submit, the Holy Spirit can fill us and enable us to love one another in a sacrificial, sanctifying, satisfying way—the way Christ loves the church.

To experience the fullness of the Spirit, a person must first possess the Spirit—be a Christian. Then there must be a sincere desire to glorify Christ, since this is why the Holy Spirit was given (John 16:14). We do not use the Holy Spirit; He uses us. There must be a deep thirst for God's fullness, a confession that we cannot do His will apart from His power. We must claim the promise of John 7:37–39: "If any man thirst, let him come unto me, and drink!" By faith yield yourself to Christ; by faith ask Him for the fullness of the Spirit. By faith receive. When you find yourself joyful, thankful, and submissive, you will know that God has answered.

One more important factor should be considered. The Spirit of God uses the Word of God to work in our lives. Read Colossians 3:16—4:1 and you will see a parallel to our Ephesians passage. And you will note that to be filled with the Word of God produces joy, thanksgiving, and submission. In other words, when you are controlled by the Word of God, you are filled with the Spirit of God. Not only husbands and wives, but all Christians need to spend time daily letting the Word of Christ dwell in them richly, for then the Spirit of God can work in our lives to make us joyful, thankful, and submissive. And this means heaven in the home—or wherever God may put us.

QUESTIONS FOR PERSONAL REFLECTION
OR GROUP DISCUSSION

1. What is one challenge to harmony that you face in your relationships?

2. Read Ephesians 5:18–33. Paul addressed the issue of harmony among believers in general and in the home specifically. What role does the Holy Spirit play in enabling us to live in harmony with others?

3. Being filled with the Spirit on an ongoing basis doesn't happen automatically; that's why Paul tells his readers to do it. What can we do to open ourselves to being filled with the Spirit?

4. Why do you suppose Paul associates gratitude (v. 20) with being filled with the Spirit?

5. How grateful of a person are you? Why is that?

6. What does it mean to be submissive to another person?

7. Why is submission to one another important to harmony?

8. Why is submission so hard for many people?

9. How do Spirit-filled husbands and wives act toward each other?

10. What is one thing you can do this week to promote harmony in your family?

Chapter Twelve

LIVING THE LORDSHIP OF CHRIST

(Ephesians 6:1–9)

After watching a television presentation about rebellious youth, a husband said to his wife, "What a mess! Where did our generation go wrong?" The wife calmly answered, "We had children."

It seems no matter where we look in modern society, we see antagonism, division, and rebellion. Husbands and wives are divorcing each other; children are rebelling against their parents; and employers and employees are seeking for new ways to avoid strikes and keep the machinery of industry running productively. We have tried education, legislation, and every other approach, but nothing seems to work. Paul's solution to the antagonisms in the home and in society was *regeneration*—a new heart from God and a new submission to Christ and to one another. God's great program is to "gather together in one all things in Christ" (Eph. 1:10). Paul indicated that this spiritual harmony begins in the lives of Christians who are submitted to the lordship of Christ.

In this section Paul admonished four groups of Christians about how they could have harmony in Christ.

1. CHRISTIAN CHILDREN (6:1–3)

Paul did not tell the parents to admonish the children; he did it himself.

Children were present in the assembly when this letter was read. Did they understand all that Paul wrote? Do *we* understand it all? Christian families attended the public worship together, and no doubt the parents explained the Word to the children when they were at home. He gave them four reasons why they should obey their parents.

(1) They are Christians ("in the Lord," v. 1a). This argument is an application of the theme of the entire section, which is "submitting yourselves one to another in the fear of God" (Eph. 5:21). When a person becomes a Christian, he is not released from normal obligations of life. If anything, his faith in Christ ought to make him a better child in the home.

To the Colossians Paul enforced his admonition with "for this is well pleasing unto the Lord" (Col. 3:20). Here is harmony in the home: The wife submits to the husband "as unto Christ"; the husband loves his wife "even as Christ also loved the church"; and the children obey "in the Lord."

(2) Obedience is right (v. 1b). There is an order in nature, ordained of God, that argues for the rightness of an action. Since the parents brought the child into the world, and since they have more knowledge and wisdom than the child, it is right that the child obey his parents. Even young animals are taught to obey. The "modern version" of Ephesians 6:1 would be, "Parents, obey your children, for this will keep them happy and bring peace to the home." But this is contrary to God's order in nature.

(3) Obedience is commanded (v. 2a). Here Paul cited the fifth commandment (Ex. 20:12; Deut. 5:16) and applies it to the New Testament believer. This does not mean that the Christian is "under the law," for Christ has set us free from both the curse and the bondage of the law (Gal. 3:13; 5:1). But the righteousness of the law is still a revelation of the holiness of God, and the Holy Spirit enables us to practice that righteousness in our daily lives (Rom. 8:1–4). All of the Ten Commandments are repeated in the New Testament Epistles for the Christian to observe except "Remember the sabbath day, to keep it holy." It is just as wrong for a New Testament Christian to dishonor his parents as it was for an Old Testament Jew.

To "honor" our parents means much more than simply to obey them. It means to show them respect and love, to care for them as long as they need us, and to seek to bring honor to them by the way we live. A young couple came to see me about getting married, and I asked if their parents agreed to the wedding. They looked at each other in embarrassment, then confessed, "We were hoping you wouldn't ask about that." I spent the next hour trying to convince them that their parents had a right to rejoice in this event, and that to exclude them would cause wounds that might never heal. "Even if they are not believers," I said, "they are your parents, and you owe them love and respect." They finally agreed, and the plans we made together made both families happy. Had we followed the couple's original plans, the two of them would have lost their testimony with their relatives, but, instead, they were able to give a good witness for Jesus Christ.

(4) Obedience brings blessing (vv. 2b–3). The fifth commandment has a promise attached to it: "That thy days may be long upon the land which the LORD thy God giveth thee" (Ex. 20:12). This promise originally applied to the Jews as they entered Canaan, but Paul applied it to believers today. He substituted "earth" for "land" and told us that the Christian child who honors his parents can expect two blessings. It will be well with him, and he will live long on the earth. This does not mean that everyone who died young dishonored his parents. He was stating a principle: When children obey their parents in the Lord, they will escape a good deal of sin and danger and thus avoid the things that could threaten or shorten their lives. But life is not measured only by quantity of time. It is also measured by quality of experience. God enriches the life of the obedient child no matter how long he may live on the earth. Sin always robs us; obedience always enriches us.

So, the child must learn early to obey father and mother, not only because they are his parents, but also because God has commanded it to be so. Disobedience to parents is rebellion against God. The sad situation in homes today is the result of rejecting God's Word (Rom. 1:28–30; 2 Tim. 3:1–5). By nature, a child is selfish, but in the power of the Holy Spirit, a child can learn to obey his parents and glorify God.

2. CHRISTIAN FATHERS (6:4)

If left to themselves, children will be rebels, so it is necessary for the parents to train their children. Years ago, the then Duke of Windsor said, "Everything in the American home is controlled by switches—except the children!" The Bible records the sad results of parents neglecting their children, either by being bad examples to them or failing to discipline them properly. David pampered Absalom and set him a bad example, and the results were tragic. Eli failed to discipline his sons, and they brought disgrace to his name and defeat to the nation of Israel. In his latter years, even Isaac pampered Esau, while his wife showed favoritism to Jacob; and the result was a divided home. Jacob was showing favoritism to Joseph when God providentially rescued the lad and made a man out of him in Egypt. Paul told us that the father has several responsibilities toward his children.

He must not provoke them. In Paul's day, the father had supreme authority over the family. When a baby was born into a Roman family, for example, it was brought out and laid before the father. If he picked it up, it meant he was accepting it into the home. But if he did not pick it up, it meant the child was rejected. It could be sold, given away, or even killed by exposure. No doubt a father's love would overcome such monstrous acts, but these practices were legal in that day. Paul told the parents, "Don't use your authority to abuse the child, but to encourage and build the child." To the Colossians he wrote, "Fathers, provoke not your children to anger, lest they be discouraged" (Col. 3:21). So, the opposite of "provoke" is "encourage."

I was addressing a group of Christian students on the subject of prayer, and was pointing out that our Father in heaven is always available when we call. To illustrate it, I told them that the receptionist at our church office has a list of names prepared by me, and these people could get to me at any time, no matter what I was doing. Even if I was in a staff meeting or in a counseling session, if any of these people phoned, she was to call me immediately. At the top of this list was my family. Even if the matter seems to me inconsequential, I want my family to know that I am available. After the service, one of the students said to me, "Would you adopt me? I can never get through to my father, and I need his encouragement so much!"

Fathers provoke their children and discourage them by saying one thing and doing another—by always blaming and never praising, by being inconsistent and unfair in discipline, and by showing favoritism in the home, by making promises and not keeping them, and by making light of problems that, to the children, are very important. Christian parents need the fullness of the Spirit so they can be sensitive to the needs and problems of their children.

He must nurture them. The text reads, "But nurture them in the discipline and admonition of the Lord." The verb translated "bring them up" is the same word that is translated "nourisheth" in Ephesians 5:29. The Christian husband is to nourish his wife and his children by sharing love and encouragement in the Lord. It is not enough to nurture the children physically by providing food, shelter, and clothing. He must also nurture them emotionally and spiritually. The development of the Boy Jesus is our example: "And Jesus increased in wisdom and stature, and in favour with God and man" (Luke 2:52). Here is balanced growth: intellectual, physical, spiritual, and social. Nowhere in the Bible is the training of children assigned to agencies outside the home, no matter how they might assist. God looks to the parents for the kind of training that the children need.

He must discipline them. The word "nurture" carries with it the idea of learning through discipline. It is translated "chastening" in Hebrews 12. Some modern psychologists oppose the old-fashioned idea of discipline, and many educators follow their philosophy. "Let the children express themselves!" they tell us. "If you discipline them, you may warp their characters." Yet discipline is a basic principle of life and an evidence of love. "Whom the Lord loveth he chasteneth" (Heb. 12:6). "He that spareth him chasteneth him diligently" (Prov. 13:24, literal translation).

We must be sure, however, that we discipline our children in the right manner. To begin with, we must discipline in love and not in anger, lest we injure either the body or the spirit of the child, or possibly both. If we are not disciplined, we surely cannot discipline others, and "flying off the handle" never made a better child or a better parent.

Also, our discipline must be fair and consistent "My father would use a cannon to kill a mosquito!" a teenager once told me. "I either get away with murder, or get blamed for everything!" Consistent, loving discipline gives assurance to the child. He may not agree with us, but at least he knows that we care enough to build some protective walls around him until he can take care of himself.

"I never knew how far I could go," a wayward girl told me, "because my parents never cared enough to discipline me. I figured that if it wasn't important to them, why should it be important to me?"

He must instruct and encourage them. This is the meaning of the word *admonition*. The father and mother not only use actions to raise the child, but also words. In the book of Proverbs, for example, we have an inspired record of a father sharing wise counsel with his son. Our children do not always appreciate our counsel, but that does not eliminate the obligation we have to instruct and encourage them. Of course, our instruction must always be tied to the Word of God (see 2 Tim. 3:13–17).

When the Supreme Court handed down its ruling against required prayer in the public schools, the famous editorial cartoonist Herblock published a cartoon in the *Washington Post* showing an angry father waving a newspaper at his family and shouting, "What do they expect us to do—listen to the kids pray at home?" The answer is yes! Home is the place where the children ought to learn about the Lord and the Christian life. It is time that Christian parents stop passing the buck to Sunday school teachers and Christian day-school teachers, and start nurturing their children.

3. Christian Servants (6:5–8)

The word *servants* undoubtedly refers to Christian slaves, but we may certainly apply these words to the Christian employee today. There were probably sixty million slaves in the Roman Empire in that day, and slavery was an accepted institution. Nowhere in the New Testament is slavery *per se* attacked or condemned, though the overall thrust of the gospel is against it. Paul's ministry was not to overthrow the Roman government or any of its institutions, but to preach the gospel and win the lost to Christ. Certainly the results of his evangelism ultimately led to the overthrow of the Roman Empire, but that was not Paul's main motive. Just as the preaching of Wesley and Whitefield resulted in the abolition of slavery and child labor, the elevation of women, and the care of the needy, so Paul's ministry contributed to the death of slavery and the encouragement of freedom. However, he was careful not to confuse the social system with the spiritual order in the church (1 Cor. 7:20–24).

Paul admonished the servants to be obedient, with several good reasons. First, they were really serving Christ. True, they had "masters according to the flesh," but their true Master was in heaven (Eph. 6:9). The fact that an employee and his employer are both Christians is no excuse for either one to do less work. Rather, it is a good reason to be more faithful to each other. The employee should show proper respect for employer, and not try to take advantage of him. He should devote his full attention and energy to the job at hand ("singleness of heart"). The best way to be a witness on the job is to do a good day's work. The Christian worker will avoid "eye service"—working only when the boss is watching, or working extra hard when he is watching, to give the impression he is doing a very good job.

The second reason is that doing a good job is the will of God. Christianity knows nothing of sacred and secular. A Christian can perform any good work as a ministry to Christ, to the glory of God. For this reason, the worker must do his job "from the heart," since he is serving Christ and doing the will of God. There were tasks assigned to these slaves that they detested, but they were to perform them just the same, so long as they were not disobeying the will of God. "Singleness of heart" and "doing the will of God from the heart" both indicate the importance of a right heart attitude on the job.

Paul's third argument is that they will be rewarded by the Lord (Eph. 6:8). In that day, slaves were treated like pieces of property, no matter how well educated they might be. An educated, cultured slave who became a Christian might receive even harsher treatment from his master because of his faith, but harsh treatment was not to keep him from doing his best (1 Peter 2:18–25). We are to serve Christ, not men. We shall receive our rewards from Christ, not from men.

4. CHRISTIAN MASTERS (6:9)

The Christian faith does not bring about harmony by erasing social or cultural distinctions. Servants are still servants when they trust Christ, and masters are still masters. Rather, the Christian faith brings harmony by working in the heart. Christ gives us a new motivation, not a new organization. Both servant and master are serving the Lord and seeking to please Him, and in this way they are able to work together to the glory of God. What are the responsibilities of a Christian master (or employer) to his workers?

He must seek their welfare. "Do the same things unto them." If the employer expects the workers to do their best for him, he must do his best for them. The master must serve the Lord from his heart if he expects his servants to do the same. He must not exploit them.

One of the greatest examples of this in the Bible is Boaz in the book of Ruth. He greeted his workers with "The Lord be with you." And they replied, "The Lord bless thee" (Ruth 2:4). Boaz was sensitive to the needs of his workers and generous to the stranger, Ruth. His relationship with his workers was one of mutual respect and a desire to glorify the Lord. It is unfortunate when an employee says, "My boss is supposed to be a Christian, but you'd never know it!"

He must not threaten. Roman masters had the power and lawful authority to kill a slave who was rebellious, though few of them did so. Slaves cost too much money to destroy them. Paul suggested that the Christian master has a better way to encourage obedience and service than threats of punishment. The negative power of fear could result in the worker doing less instead of more, and this kind of motivation could not be continued over a long period of time. Far better was the positive motivation of "that which is just and equal" (Col. 4:1). Let a man share the results of his labor and he will work better and harder. Even the Old Testament gives this same counsel: "Thou shalt not rule over him with rigour, but shalt fear thy God" (Lev. 25:43).

He must be submitted to the Lord. "Your master also is in heaven" (Eph. 6:9). This is practicing the lordship of Christ. The wife submits to her own husband "as unto the Lord" (Eph. 5:22), and the husband loves the wife "as Christ also loved the church" (Eph. 5:25). Children obey their parents "in the Lord" (Eph. 6:1), and parents raise their children "in the nurture and admonition of the Lord" (Eph. 6:4). Servants are obedient "as unto Christ" (Eph. 6:5), and masters treat their servants as their "Master in heaven" would have them do. Each person, in submission to the Lord, has no problems submitting to those over him.

Jesus said the way to be a ruler is first to be a servant (Matt. 25:21). The person who is not under authority has no right to exercise authority. This explains why many of the great men of the Bible were first servants before God made them rulers: Joseph, Moses, Joshua, David, and Nehemiah are just a few examples. Even after a man becomes a leader, he must still lead by serving. An African proverb says, "The chief is servant of all." "And whosoever will be chief among you, let him be your servant" (Matt. 20:27).

A friend of mine was promoted to a place of executive leadership and, unfortunately, it went to his head. He enjoyed all of his executive privileges and more, and never lost an opportunity to remind his employees who was in charge. But he lost the respect of his workers, and production and efficiency went down so fast that the board had to replace him. Because my friend forgot that he had a "Master in heaven," he failed to be a good "master on earth."

He must not play favorites. God is no respecter of persons. He will judge a master or a servant if he sins, or He will reward a master or a servant if he obeys (Eph. 6:8). A Christian employer cannot take privileges with God simply because of his position; nor should a Christian employer play favorites with those under his authority. Paul warned Timothy to "observe these things without preferring one before another, doing nothing by partiality" (1 Tim. 5:21). One of the fastest ways for a leader to divide his followers and lose their confidence is for the leader to play favorites and show partiality.

This closes the section we have called "Walk in Harmony." If we are filled with the Holy Spirit and are joyful, thankful, and submissive, then we can enjoy harmony in the relationships of life as we live and work with other Christians. We will also find it easier to work with and witness to the unbelievers who may disagree with us. The fruit of the Spirit is love, and love is the greatest adhesive in the world!

QUESTIONS FOR PERSONAL REFLECTION
OR GROUP DISCUSSION

1. How easy or difficult is it for you to obey someone in authority over you? Why?

2. Read Ephesians 6:1–9. What does it mean for young children to honor their parents? What about adult children?

3. How can fathers avoid provoking their children to wrath?

4. How can fathers nurture and instruct their children instead? Give some examples.

5. How much time and energy do you think it takes for fathers to do what Paul urges? How does this affect the father's investment in his career or his other interests?

6. What motivations did Paul give servants for obeying their masters?

7. What motivations did he give masters for treating their servants well?

8. How is all this relevant to employers and employees today?

9. In what specific ways can you produce harmony with other Christians this week?

Chapter Thirteen

You're in the Army Now!

(Ephesians 6:10–24)

S ooner or later every believer discovers that the Christian life is a battle-ground, not a playground, and that he faces an enemy who is much stronger than he is—apart from the Lord. That Paul should use the military to illustrate the believer's conflict with Satan is reasonable. He himself was chained to a Roman soldier (Eph. 6:20), and his readers were certainly familiar with soldiers and the equipment they used. In fact, military illustrations were favorites with Paul (2 Cor. 10:4; 1 Tim. 6:12; 2 Tim. 2:3; 4:7).

As Christians, we face three enemies: the world, the flesh, and the Devil (Eph. 2:1–3). "The world" refers to the system around us that is opposed to God, that caters to "the lust of the flesh, and the lust of the eyes, and the pride of life" (1 John 2:15–17). "Society apart from God" is a simple, but accurate, definition of "the world." "The flesh" is the old nature that we inherited from Adam, a nature that is opposed to God and can do nothing spiritual to please God. By His death and resurrection, Christ overcame the world (John 16:33; Gal. 6:14), and the flesh (Rom. 6:1–6; Gal. 2:20), and the Devil (Eph. 1:19–23). In other words, as believers, we do not fight *for* victory—we fight *from* victory! The Spirit of God enables us, by faith, to appropriate Christ's victory for ourselves.

In these closing verses of the letter, Paul discussed four topics so that his readers, by understanding and applying these truths, might walk in victory.

1. THE ENEMY (6:10–12)

The intelligence corps plays a vital part in warfare because it enables the officers to know and understand the enemy. Unless we know who the enemy is, where he is, and what he can do, we have a difficult time defeating him. Not only in Ephesians 6, but throughout the entire Bible, God instructs us about the enemy, so there is no reason for us to be caught off guard.

The leader—the Devil. The enemy has many different names. *Devil* means "accuser," because he accuses God's people day and night before the throne of God (Rev. 12:7–11). *Satan* means "adversary," because he is the enemy of God. He is also called the tempter (Matt. 4:3), and the murderer and the liar (John 8:44). He is compared to a lion (1 Peter 5:8), a serpent (Gen. 3:1; Rev. 12:9), and an angel of light (2 Cor. 11:13–15), as well as "the god of this age" (2 Cor. 4:4 NIV).

Where did he come from, this spirit-creature that seeks to oppose God and defeat His work? Many students believe that in the original creation, he was "Lucifer, son of the morning" (Isa. 14:12–15) and that he was cast down because of his pride and his desire to occupy God's throne. Many mysteries are connected with the origin of Satan, but what he is doing and where he is going are certainly no mystery! Since he is a created being, and not eternal (as God is), he is limited in his knowledge and activity. Unlike God, Satan is not all-knowing, all-powerful, or everywhere-present. Then how does he accomplish so much in so many different parts of the world? The answer is in his organized helpers.

Satan's helpers. Paul called them "principalities … powers … rulers … spiritual wickedness in high places" (Eph. 6:12). Charles B. Williams translated it, "For our contest is not with human foes alone, but with the rulers, authorities, and cosmic powers of this dark world; that is, with the spirit forces of evil challenging us in the heavenly contest" (WMS). This suggests a definite army of demonic creatures that assist Satan in his attacks against believers. The apostle John hinted that one third of the angels fell with Satan when he rebelled against God (Rev. 12:4), and Daniel wrote that Satan's angels struggle against God's angels for control of the affairs of nations (Dan. 10:13–20). A spiritual battle is going on in this world and in the sphere of "the heavenlies," and you and I are a part of this battle. Knowing this makes "walking in victory" a vitally important thing to us—and to God.

The important point is that our battle is not against human beings. It is against spiritual powers. We are wasting our time fighting people when we ought to be fighting the Devil, who seeks to control people and make them oppose the work of God. During Paul's ministry in Ephesus, a riot took place that could have destroyed the church (Acts 19:21–41). It wasn't caused only by Demetrius and his associates, for behind them were Satan and his associates. Certainly Paul and the church prayed, and the opposition was silenced. The advice of the king of Syria to his soldiers can be applied to our spiritual battle: "Fight neither with small nor great, save only with the king" (1 Kings 22:31).

Satan's abilities. The admonitions Paul gave indicate that Satan is a strong enemy (Eph. 6:10–12) and that we need the power of God to be able to stand against him. Never underestimate the power of the Devil. He is not compared to a lion and a dragon just for fun! The book of Job tells what his power can do to a man's body, home, wealth, and friends. Jesus called Satan a thief who comes "to steal, and to kill, and to destroy" (John 10:10). Not only is Satan strong, but he is also wise and subtle, and we fight against "the wiles of the devil." *Wiles* means "cunning, crafty arts, strategems." The Christian cannot afford to be "ignorant of his devices" (2 Cor. 2:11). Some men are cunning and crafty and "lie in wait to deceive" (Eph. 4:14), but behind them is the arch-deceiver, Satan. He masquerades as an angel of light (2 Cor. 11:14) and seeks to blind men's minds to the truth of God's Word. The fact that Paul uses the word *wrestle* indicates that we are involved in a hand-to-hand battle and are not mere spectators at a game. Satan wants to use our external enemy, the world, and our internal enemy, the flesh, to defeat us. His weapons and battle plans are formidable.

2. The Equipment (6:13–17)

Since we are fighting against enemies in the spirit world, we need special equipment both for offense and defense. God has provided the "whole armor" for us, and we dare not omit any part. Satan looks for that unguarded area where he can get a beachhead (Eph. 4:27). Paul commanded his readers to put on the armor, take the weapons, and withstand Satan, all of which we do by faith. Knowing that Christ has already conquered Satan, and that the spiritual armor and weapons are available, by faith we accept what God gives us and go out to meet the foe. The day is evil, and the enemy is evil, but "If God be for us, who can be against us?" (Rom. 8:31).

The girdle of truth (v. 14a). Satan is a liar (John 8:44), but the believer whose life is controlled by truth will defeat him. The girdle held the other parts of the armor together, and truth is the integrating force in the life of the victorious Christian. A man of integrity, with a clear conscience, can face the enemy without fear. The girdle also held the sword. Unless we practice the truth, we cannot use the Word of truth. Once a lie gets into the life of a believer, everything begins to fall apart. For over a year, King David lied about his sin with Bathsheba, and nothing went right. Psalms 32 and 51 tell of the price he paid.

The breastplace of righteousness (v. 14b). This piece of armor, made of metal plates or chains, covered the body from the neck to the waist, both front and back. It symbolizes the believer's righteousness in Christ (2 Cor. 5:21) as well as his righteous life in Christ (Eph. 4:24). Satan is the accuser, but he cannot accuse the believer who is living a godly life in the power of the Spirit. The life we live either fortifies us against Satan's attacks or makes it easier for him to defeat us (2 Cor. 6:1–10). When Satan accuses the Christian, it is the righteousness of Christ that assures the believer of his salvation. But our positional righteousness in Christ, without practical righteousness in the daily life, only gives Satan opportunity to attack us.

The shoes of the gospel (v. 15). The Roman soldier wore sandals with hobnails in the soles to give him better footing for the battle. If we are going to "stand" and "withstand," then we need the shoes of the gospel. Because we have the peace with God (Rom. 5:1) that comes from the gospel, we need not fear the attack of Satan or men. We must be at peace with God and with each other if we are to defeat the Devil (James 4:1–7). But the shoes have another meaning. We must be prepared each day to share the gospel of peace with a lost world. The most victorious Christian is a witnessing Christian. If we wear the shoes of the gospel, then we have the "beautiful feet" mentioned in Isaiah 52:7 and Romans 10:15. Satan has declared war, but you and I are ambassadors of peace (2 Cor. 5:18–21); and, as such, we take the gospel of peace wherever we go.

The shield of faith (v. 16). The shield was large, usually about four feet by two feet, made of wood, and covered with tough leather. As the soldier held it before him, it protected him from spears, arrows, and "fiery darts." The edges of these shields were so constructed that an entire line of soldiers could interlock shields and march into the enemy like a solid wall. This suggests that we Christians are not in the battle alone. The "faith" mentioned here is not saving faith, but rather living faith, a trust in the promises and the power of God. Faith is a defensive weapon that protects us from Satan's fiery darts. In Paul's day, arrows, dipped in some inflammable substance and ignited, were shot at the enemy. Satan shoots "fiery darts" at our hearts and minds: lies, blasphemous thoughts, hateful thoughts about others, doubts, and burning desires for sin. If we do not by faith quench these darts, they will light a fire within and we will disobey God. We never know when Satan will shoot a dart at us, so we must always walk by faith and use the shield of faith.

The helmet of salvation (v. 17). Satan wants to attack the mind, the way he defeated Eve (Gen. 3; 2 Cor. 11:1–3). The helmet refers to the mind controlled by God. It is too bad that many Christians have the idea that the intellect is not important, when in reality it plays a vital role in Christian growth, service, and victory. When God controls the mind, Satan cannot lead the believer astray. The Christian who studies his Bible and learns the meaning of Bible doctrines is not going to be led astray too easily. We need to be "taught by him, as the truth is in Jesus" (Eph. 4:21). We are to "grow in grace, and in the knowledge of our Lord and Saviour Jesus Christ" (2 Peter 3:18). Wherever Paul ministered, he taught the new converts the truths of the Word of God, and this helmet protected them from Satan's lies.

One Sunday afternoon, I visited a man who had been a deacon in a local church, but was at that time involved in a false cult. We sat at the table with open Bibles, and I tried to show him the truth of God's Word, but it seemed his mind was blinded by lies. "How did you happen to turn away from a Bible-preaching church and get involved in this belief?" I asked, and his reply stunned me.

"Preacher, I blame the church. I didn't know anything about the Bible, and they didn't teach me much more. I wanted to study the Bible, but nobody told me how. Then they made me a deacon, and I wasn't ready for it. It was too much for me. I heard this man preaching the Bible over the radio and it sounded as if he knew something. I started reading his magazine and studying his books, and now I'm convinced he's right."

What a tragedy that when his local church took him in, they failed to fit him with the helmet of salvation. Had they practiced the truth found in 2 Timothy 2:2, this man might not have been a casualty in the battle.

The sword of the Spirit (v. 17b). This sword is the offensive weapon God provides us. The Roman soldier wore on his girdle a short sword which was used for close-in fighting. Hebrews 4:12 compares the Word of God to a sword, because it is sharp and is able to pierce the inner man just as a material sword pierces the body. You and I were "cut to the heart" (Acts 2:37; 5:33) when the Word convicted us of our sins. Peter tried to use a sword to defend Jesus in the garden (Luke 22:47–51), but he learned at Pentecost that the "sword of the Spirit" does a much better job. Moses also tried to conquer with a physical sword (Ex. 2:11–15), only to discover that God's Word alone was more than enough to defeat Egypt.

A material sword pierces the body, but the Word of God pierces the heart. The more you use a physical sword, the duller it becomes, but using God's Word only makes it sharper in our lives. A physical sword requires the hand of a soldier, but the sword of the Spirit has its own power, for it is "living and powerful" (Heb. 4:12). The Spirit wrote the Word, and the Spirit wields the Word as we take it by faith and use it. A physical sword wounds to hurt and kill, while the sword of the Spirit wounds to heal and give life. But when we use the sword against Satan, we are out to deal him a blow that will cripple him and keep him from hindering God's work.

When He was tempted by Satan in the wilderness, Christ used the sword of the Spirit and defeated the enemy. Three times Jesus said, "It is written" (Luke 4:1–13). Note that Satan can also quote the Word—"For it is written" (Luke 4:10)—but he does not quote it completely. Satan tries to use the Word of God to confuse us, so it is important that we know every word that God has given us. "You can prove anything by the Bible," someone said. True—if you take verses out of context, leave out words, and apply verses to Christians today that do not really apply. The better you know the Word of God, the easier it will be for you to detect Satan's lies and reject his offers.

In one sense, the "whole armor of God" is a picture of Jesus Christ. Christ is the Truth (John 14:6), and He is our righteousness (2 Cor. 5:21) and our peace (Eph. 2:14). His faithfulness makes possible our faith (Gal. 2:20); He is our salvation (Luke 2:30); and He is the Word of God (John 1:1, 14). This means that when we trusted Christ, we received the armor. Paul told the Romans what to do with the armor (Rom. 13:11–14): Wake up (Rom. 13:11), cast off sin, and "put on the armour of light" (Rom. 13:12). We do this by putting "on the Lord Jesus Christ" (Rom. 13:14). By faith, put on the armor and trust God for the victory. Once and for all, we have put on the armor at the moment of salvation. But there must be a daily appropriation. When King David put off his armor and returned to his palace, he was in greater danger than when he was on the battlefield (2 Sam. 11). We are never out of reach of Satan's devices, so we must never be without the whole armor of God.

3. THE ENERGY (6:18–20)

Prayer is the energy that enables the Christian soldier to wear the armor and wield the sword. We cannot fight the battle in our own power, no matter how strong or talented we may think we are. When Amalek attacked Israel, Moses went to the mountaintop to pray, while Joshua used the sword down in the valley (Ex. 17:8–16). It took both to defeat Amalek—Moses' intercession on the mountain and Joshua's use of the sword in the valley. Prayer is the power for victory, but not just any kind of prayer. Paul told how to pray if we would defeat Satan.

Pray always. This obviously does not mean "always saying prayers." We are not heard for our "much speaking" (Matt. 6:7). "Pray without ceasing" (1 Thess. 5:17) says to us, "Always be in communion with the Lord. Keep the receiver off the hook!" Never have to say when you pray, "Lord, we come into Thy presence," because you never left His presence! A Christian must "pray always" because he is always subject to temptations and attacks of the Devil. A surprise attack has defeated more than one believer who forgot to "pray without ceasing."

Pray with all prayer. There is more than one kind of praying: prayer, supplication, intercession, thanksgiving (Phil. 4:6; 1 Tim. 2:1). The believer who prays only to ask for things is missing out on blessings that come with intercessions and giving of thanks. In fact, thanksgiving is a great prayer weapon for defeating Satan. "Praise changes things" as much as "prayer changes things." Intercession for others can bring victory to our own lives. "And the LORD turned the captivity of Job, when he prayed for his friends" (Job 42:10).

Pray in the Spirit. The Bible formula is that we pray to the Father, through the Son, and in the Spirit. Romans 8:26–27 tells us that only in the Spirit's power can we pray in the will of God. Otherwise, our praying could be selfish and out of the will of God. In the Old Testament tabernacle, there was a small golden altar standing before the veil, and here the priest burned the incense (Ex. 30:1–10; Luke 1:1–11). The incense is a picture of prayer. It had to be mixed according to God's plan and could not be counterfeited by man. The fire on the altar is a picture of the Holy Spirit, for it is He who takes our prayers and "ignites" them in the will of God. It is possible to pray fervently in the flesh and never get through to God. It is also possible to pray quietly in the Spirit and see God's hand do great things.

Pray with your eyes open. *Watching* means "keeping on the alert." The phrase "watch and pray" occurs often in the Bible. When Nehemiah was repairing the walls of Jerusalem and the enemy was trying to stop the work, Nehemiah defeated the enemy by watching and praying. "Nevertheless we made our prayer unto our God, and set a watch" (Neh. 4:9). "Watch and pray" is the secret of victory over the world (Mark 13:33), the flesh (Mark 14:38), and the Devil (Eph. 6:18). Peter went to sleep when he should have been praying, and the result was victory for Satan (Mark 14:29–31, 67–72). God expects us to use our God-given senses, led by the Spirit, so that we detect Satan when he is beginning to work.

Keep on praying. The word *perseverance* simply means "to stick to it and not quit." The early believers prayed this way (Acts 1:14; 2:42; 6:4), and we also should pray this way (Rom. 12:12). Perseverance in prayer does not mean we are trying to twist God's arm, but rather that we are deeply concerned and burdened and cannot rest until we get God's answer. As Robert Law put it, "Prayer is not getting man's will done in heaven; it is getting God's will done on earth" (*Tests of Life,* [Baker, 1968]). Most of us quit praying just before God is about to give the victory. Not everybody is so constituted that he can sincerely spend a whole night in prayer, but all of us can persevere in prayer far more than we do. The early church prayed without ceasing when Peter was in prison and, at the last moment, God gave them their answer (Acts 12:1–19). Keep on praying until the Spirit stops you or the Father answers you. Just about the time you feel like quitting, God will give the answer.

Pray for all the saints. The Lord's Prayer begins with "Our Father"— not "My Father." We pray as part of a great family that is also talking to God, and we ought to pray for the other members of the family. Even Paul asked for the prayer support of the Ephesians—and he had been to the third heaven and back. If Paul needed the prayers of the saints, how much more do you and I need them! If my prayers help another believer defeat Satan, then that victory will help me too. Note that Paul did not ask them to pray for his comfort or safety, but for the effectiveness of his witness and ministry.

4. THE ENCOURAGEMENT (6:21–24)

We are not fighting the battle alone. There are other believers who stand with us in the fight, and we ought to be careful to encourage one another. Paul encouraged the Ephesians; Tychicus was an encouragement to Paul (Acts 20:4); and Paul was going to send Tychicus to Ephesus to be an encouragement to them. Paul was not the kind of missionary who kept his affairs to himself. He wanted the people of God to know what God was doing, how their prayers were being answered, and what Satan was doing to oppose the work. His motive was not selfish. He was not trying to get something out of them.

What an encouragement it is to be a part of the family of God! Nowhere in the New Testament do we find an isolated believer. Christians are like sheep; they flock together. The church is an army, and the soldiers need to stand together and fight together.

Note the words Paul used as he closed this letter: peace—love—faith—grace! He was a prisoner of Rome, yet he was richer than the emperor. No matter what our circumstances may be, in Jesus Christ we are "blessed with all spiritual blessings"!

QUESTIONS FOR PERSONAL REFLECTION
OR GROUP DISCUSSION

1. "The Christian life is a battleground, not a playground." Do you agree or disagree with this statement? Why?

2. Read Ephesians 6:10–24. This passage goes back to the theme of power and strength that we've seen before. What does Paul say about those things here?

3. What are some of the Devil's schemes that Paul refers to in verse 11?

4. In what ways do you experience the battle Paul talks about?

5. How is each of the pieces of armor helpful to you in standing against the Devil's schemes?

6. Which one of the pieces of armor or weapons do you need to pay more attention to? Explain.

7. What have you learned from this study of Ephesians that has affected you the most?

8. What will you do differently as a result of this study?

The "BE" series . . .

For years pastors and lay leaders have embraced Warren W. Wiersbe's very accessible commentary of the Bible through the individual "BE" series. Through the work of David C. Cook Global Mission, the "BE" series is part of a library of books made available to indigenous Christian workers. These are men and women who are called by God to grow the kingdom through their work with the local church worldwide. Here are a few of their remarks as to how Dr. Wiersbe's writings have benefited their ministry.

"Most Christian books I see are priced too high for me . . .
I received a collection that included 12 Wiersbe
commentaries a few months ago and I have
read every one of them.
I use them for my personal devotions every day and they
are incredibly helpful for preparing sermons.
The contribution David C. Cook is making to the
church in India is amazing."
—Pastor E. M. Abraham, Hyderabad, India

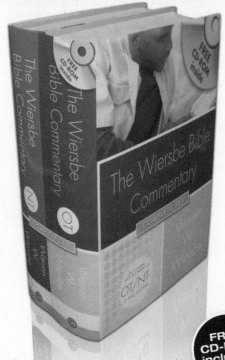